TRAINING TECHNIQUES AND METHODS

TRAINING TECHNIQUES AND METHODS

By

Prof. S. Nakkiran
Professor
Department of Cooperatives
Institute of Cooperatives & Development Studies
Ambo University
Ambo, Ethiopia
Email: doctorsnakkiran@gmail.com
&
Dr. M. Karthikeyan
Assistant Professor
Department of Cooperatives
Faculty of Business & Economics
Hawassa University
Hawassa
Email: mkeya2003@gmail.com
mkeya2003@yahoo.com

DPH

DISCOVERY PUBLISHING HOUSE PVT. LTD.
NEW DELHI-110 002

Published by:

Tilak Wasan

DISCOVERY PUBLISHING HOUSE PVT. LTD.

4383/4A, Ansari Road, Darya Ganj

New Delhi-110 002 (India)

Phone : +91-11-23279245, 43596064-65

Fax : +91-11-23253475

E-mail : parul.wasan@gmail.com
discoverypublishinghouse@gmail.com

web : www.discoverypublishinggroup.com

***First Edition:* 2012**

ISBN: 978-93-5056-124-9

Training Techniques and Methods

Printed at:

Shree Balaji Art Press

Delhi

Preface

Dear Learners! It is our pleasure to introduce the textbook *Training Techniques and Methods* to you. This book is devoted to the enrichment of training materials for the modern managers. Training and development are continuous process in improving the calibres of managers and executives. Having this in mind, we have completed this work.

Though number of literature has come out on training and development, the present work is a concrete and precious one, in the sense it can accommodate the readers through theoretical and practical connotations. This book will be very useful to the practicing managers, the trainers who are working in various training establishments and the students of management at undergraduate and M.B.A and similar post-graduate levels and professionals involved in cooperative departments.

This work is based on our experience as teachers, trainers and researchers in the field of cooperatives. The present work is based on the outcome of our teaching and research experience, articles published in reputed journals, and discussions with public, private and cooperative officials. We have drawn the inputs from various materials— papers, journals, books, websites and we have consulted several of our friends, colleagues and field experts. We are ever grateful and thankful to them for their immense support and healthy criticism. We hope that the readers of this book will get theoretical and practical knowledge on training techniques and methods. Any useful comments, suggestions to improve the present version are welcome and solicited from the readers. We are thankful and grateful to Parul Wasan, Discovery Publishing House Pvt. Ltd., New Delhi for publishing the book neatly under his renowned label for the cooperative knowledge community.

S. NAKKIRAN

M. KARTHIKEYAN

CONTENTS

1

TRAINING AND DEVELOPMENT

Definition of Training

According to Dale Beach: "Training is the organized procedure by which people learn knowledge and/or skills for a definite purpose".

Steinnets defines as: "A short term process utilizing a systematic and organized procedure by which non-managerial personnel learn technical knowledge and the skills for a definite purpose".

Meaning of Training

Training is an attempt to improve the current or future performance of an employee. The meaning of training is as follows:

1. Training is a systematic process of altering the behaviour of employees in a direction to increase the organization goals.
2. A training programme is an effort by the employer to provide opportunities for the employee to acquire job related skills, attitudes, and knowledge.
3. Training must result in permanent change in the behaviour of an individual through learning.
4. Another meaning of training is the skills improvement for an employee.

- Training is the transfer of defined and measurable knowledge or skill. Training activities should have objectives and a method for checking whether these objectives have been met. While it is essential to have a training facility, policy and standards, it is necessary to define it clearly by the organization.

Training is basically learning. Training can be seen as an attempt by the organization to change the behaviour of its members through the learning process in order to increase effectiveness. Training programmes are directed towards maintaining and improving current job performance. On the other hand, development programmes seek to develop skills for future jobs. Both managers and non-managers may receive training and development programmes, but the mix of experience is likely to vary. Non-managers are much more likely to be trained in the technical skills required for their current jobs, whereas managers receive assistance in developing the skills required for the future job. The working definition of training is "Training is the transfer of defined and measurable knowledge or skills". From this definition, it can be seen that training activities should have objectives and methods for checking whether these objectives have been met.

Management Development

Management development is designed to improve the overall effectiveness of managers in their present positions and to prepare them for greater responsibility when they are promoted. Management development programmes have become more prevalent in recent years because of increasingly complex demands on managers and because training managers through experience alone is a time consuming process. New employees usually already have the educational training needed to perform the basics of a new job. Managers must begin with that level of development and build on it through additional training and development. Hence, training may be defined as attaining specific, detailed, and routine job skills and techniques. Development is the broad scope of improvement and growth of abilities, attitudes, and personality traits.

Table 1.1: Distinction between Training and Development

Sl. No.	Training	Development
1.	Training is concerned with teaching technical skills.	Development is concerned with teaching technical, human, and conceptual skills.
2.	Training is useful in the case of non-managerial personnel.	Development is useful in the case of managerial personnel.
3.	Training seeks to develop skills already possessed by workers.	Development seeks to develop hidden qualities and talent of personnel.
4.	Training makes use of on-the-job training methods such as apprenticeship, assistant to positions, vestibule training, etc.	Development makes use of off-the-job training methods such as job rotation, lecture, role play, etc.
5.	Training seeks to make workers proficient in their existing jobs	Development seeks to prepare employees for handling more responsible and challenging jobs.

Types of Training

Training can be divided into the following types:

1. *Induction Training:* When a new employee is selected, he has to be placed on a job. To make sure that initial placement of the employee is faultless, induction training is essential. Such programme may include tour of the whole plant, supplying information about the company, products of the firm, rules, regulations, etc.
2. *Job Training:* It is given in different ways to make the worker proficient in handling machines, equipments, and materials, so that operations are smooth and faultless.
3. *Craft Training:* It involves the preparation not for a single job but for many types of related jobs, which can be assigned to a competent craftsman.
4. *Promotion Training:* When an existing employee is promoted within the organization, to equip him to the new job, some training in both better skill and knowledge is given.
5. *Refresher Training:* An employee might have got an initial training, but in course of time such training may be outdated in terms of the job. Re-training programmes are designed to avoid personal obsolescence.

Subject Matter and Course Content of Training

1. *Company or the organization*
   - *(a)* Objectives and philosophy
   - *(b)* Policies and procedure
   - *(c)* Products and services
   - *(d)* Organizational structure and organizational dynamics
   - *(e)* Plant facilities
   - *(f)* Financial picture
   - *(g)* The labour agreement and union management relations

Table 1.2: Skills Taught in Various Types of Training

Type	Skills
Interpersonal skills	Leadership, couching, communication skills, conflict resolution, team building, customer service, diversity and cultural awareness, sales process
Technical	Product training and knowledge, sales process, information technology, computer application, other technical skills necessary to do a particular job
Business	Finance, marketing, manufacturing, quality, strategic planning, organizational culture
Mandatory	Safety, health, sexual harassment, and other legal compliance
Performance management	Any training to help an individual to improve his work performance
Problem solving/Decision-making	Defining problems, assessing causation, creativity in developing alternatives, analyzing alternatives, selecting solution
Personal	Career planning, time management, personal finance or money management, public speaking

2. *Management principles and techniques*
   - *(a)* Organization principles
   - *(b)* Financial planning and management
   - *(c)* Management information systems
   - *(d)* Production planning and control
   - *(e)* Methods analysis and work measurement
   - *(f)* Personnel management
   - *(g)* Wage and salary administration
   - *(h)* Cost analysis and control
   - *(i)* Statistics and probability
   - *(j)* Operations research
   - *(k)* Data processing and computers
   - *(l)* Marketing
   - *(m)* Risk management
3. *Human relations*
   - *(a)* Fundamentals of human behaviour
   - *(b)* Motivation
   - *(c)* Group dynamics
   - *(d)* Attitudes
   - *(e)* Conflict resolution
   - *(f)* Managing change
   - *(g)* Patters of management
   - *(h)* Concepts of leadership
   - *(i)* Power, authority, influence
   - *(j)* Communication
   - *(k)* Personnel management responsibilities of supervision in such areas as selection, training, pay administration, counseling appraisal, discipline, and grievance handling
4. *Technical knowledge and skills*

(a) To create adequate understanding of the technology, products, processes, and methods of business.

5. *Economic, social and political environment*
   - *(a)* Business ethics
   - *(b)* Economic system
   - *(c)* Relations with local, state and federal governments
   - *(d)* Community relations
   - *(e)* Social responsibilities
   - *(f)* Legal framework for business
   - *(g)* Business operations in foreign countries
   - *(h)* Environmental issues
   - *(i)* Consumerism
6. *Personal skills*
   - *(a)* Speaking
   - *(b)* Report writing
   - *(c)* Conducting meetings
   - *(d)* Reading improvement
   - *(e)* Interpersonal skills, listening, feedback, communication

Courses for Various Levels of Management

Courses for top management will emphasize such subjects as economics, finance, organization theory, human relations, policy formulation, administrative controls, business operations overseas, the business person in politics, labor relations, and public relations.

Courses for middle management contain elements of both top and lower management programmes. They devote considerable time to human relations and personnel management principles because they are essential at all levels of management. They must possess solid grounding in such grounding techniques as cost analysis and control, data processing, production planning and control, and wage and salary administration.

Courses for lower level management concentrate upon technical processes of the business, human relations, and personal skills. They tend to be immediately practical. They are closely related to the supervisor's day-to-day job.

Kinds of Change Induced by Training

1. *The change in behaviour:* This includes change in the behaviour of an employee at all levels. It also includes change in how we interact with our peers.
2. *Transmitting information:* Training programmes transmit new information to the trainees. People are shown where they work, what their job is and who to contact about different issues and are briefed about the rules and regulations.
3. *Development of attitudes:* Closely linked to the imparting of knowledge is the development of attitudes. People enter training programmes with many pre-conceived notions on training, their job, etc. It is important to change these attitudes to make the programme successful.
4. *Development of skills:* In a training programme considerable amount of information has been transmitted and in the process of training their attitudes have been changed. In addition to that, they are taught skill development, which is derived from on-the-job training. Classroom situation of human problems through case studies and role playing can be practiced.
5. *Conceptual changes:* Behavioural science has developed a number of conclusions about human personality, motivation, communication, group process and leadership. The learning and application of these general rules involves learning of new information, attitude and skill. Basic beliefs and attitudes about what causes behaviour need to be changed and the actual problem solving skills need to be modified. A trainee needs to behave differently in response to the problem.

Training Activities

The following activities are considered as training:

1. Classroom (trainer led)

2. Distance learning
3. Computer-based training
4. On-the-job training
5. External courses
6. Workshops and seminars
7. Attending exhibitions
8. Evening classes
9. Participating in quality circles
10. Reading articles and books

The French Ministry of Work, Employment, and Professional Training considers the training activities as follows:

1. Has predetermined objectives
2. Specifies the teaching methods
3. Specifies the personnel to be used
4. Has an implementation plant
5. Assess the results
6. Is given premises separate from the production area unless it includes practical training
7. Can include correspondence courses, safety, and security training and training outside of working hours.

Goals of Training

1. *Training validity:* Did the trainees learn skills or acquire knowledge or abilities during the training?
2. *Transfer validity:* Did the knowledge, skills, or abilities learned in training led to the improved performance on the job?
3. *Intra-organizational validity:* Is the job performance of a new group of trainees in the same organization that developed the programme comparable with the job performance of the original training groups?
4. *Inter-organizational validity:* Can a training programme that has been validated in one organization be used successfully in another firm?

Main Areas in which Training can Operate

1. *Knowledge:* Through training we are helping the trainee to learn, to understand, and to remember facts, information, and principles.
2. *Skills:* A skill is a physical act or action. Examples are operating a machine, shorthand writing, etc.
3. *Techniques:* A technique usually involves the application in a dynamic situation of both knowledge and skill. It is the way of behaviour or thinking.
4. *Attitude:* The trainer have the ability to properly diagnose the attitudes or the knowledge and skill with which to seek the change.
5. *Experience:* It is the result of practicing the use of knowledge, skills, and techniques over a period of time in a number of difficult situations. This is achieved by means of job rotation and sometimes by exchanges between companies.

Skills Taught in Training

1. *Communication:* Every training is in need of acquiring communication skills. An effective training can teach good communication methods and procedures. Trainees will also be given various courses relating to training.
2. *Computer skills:* This is an age of computers. Every employee from the lower level to top level is expected to know the various aspects of computer. They should also be given training relating to computer skills, which are relevant to their work.
3. *Customer service:* In the competitive world customer attraction and customer service are the slogans for organizations. Employee must be taught various methods of customer services through effective training.
4. *Diversity of views:* An employee must be trained to look at and analyze a problem from various angles. Such diversity can help an employee to choose the right method to solve a problem.

5. *Ethics:* Along with good human characters, an employee must possess personal ethics of honesty, hard work, friendliness, clean-handedness, etc. These must also be taught during the training period.
6. *Human relations:* A human relation is the connecting link to have effective organizational enrichment. A human relation is needed between one employee and another employee, between an employee and customer, which can be taught during training periods.
7. *Quality initiative:* Inculcating quality in all aspects of the organization is a precondition for an employee. They have to join their hands with the organization in improving the quality of service, quality of product and quality of the organization.
8. *Safety:* An employee must be trained in the safety measures relating to the organization. Factory safety, as well as safety in public places must also be taught during the training period.
9. *Knowledge:* In addition to skills the trainee must learn new knowledge. A training exercise can teach them way of acquiring new knowledge.
10. *Attitude:* Employees must cultivate right attitude towards their superiors and subordinates, towards customers and towards public. These must also be taught during training period.

Summary

- Training is basically learning. Training can be seen as an attempt by the organization to change the behaviour of its members through the learning process in order to increase effectiveness. Training programmes are directed towards maintaining and improving current job performance.
- There are different types of training; various required skills are taught in training.

Self-Learning Activity

Try to answer the following questions on your own:

1. Define training?
2. What are the different types of training?
3. Give an account of skills taught in training.

2

MANAGER AND MANAGEMENT DEVELOPMENT

The word manager has been used in a variety of ways by others. To some, the term manager means top executive, to others a manager is any person who supervises other employees. But the organizational structure of a firm contains number of echelons, each level possessing the designation of manager. In every sense, a manager is a key person and responsible for the day-to-day affairs and for the ultimate success of an organization. One way of understanding what manager do is to examine the functions of management. The process of management consists of planning, organizing, staffing, directing, and controlling. Planning comprises of looking ahead of the future, setting goals, and figuring out policies, procedures, and methods of achieving these goals. The decision-making process forms the important process of planning. Organizing involves the breaking down of the total work to be done into jobs, groups, and departments and establishment of workable relationships between these units. It includes such elements as grouping of activities, setting-up jobs, determining authority and responsibility relationships, setting-up patterns of communication, delegating and the use of staff. Staffing refers to the process of recruiting and selecting people to run the enterprise. Direction is the motivation and leading people to achieve the desired goal. It integrates the personal goals of the employees with the objectives of the enterprise. The control function includes measurement of work performed, comparison of actual performance with a predetermined standard and taking corrective action to ensure that performance meets standard.

Skills Needed for Managers

According to Robert Katz, the following skills are needed by managers:

1. *Technical skill:* It is knowledge of and proficiencies in activities involving methods, process, and procedures. Thus, it involves working with tools and specific techniques.
2. *Human skill:* It is the ability to work with people, it is cooperative effort, it is team work, and it is the creation of an environment in which people feel secured and free to express their opinions.
3. *Conceptual skill:* This refers to the ability to see the "big picture", to recognize significant elements in a situation, to understand the relationships among the elements.
4. *Design skill:* This refers to the ability to solve problems that will benefit the enterprise. To be effective, managers must be able to do more than see a problem. Managers must also have the valuable skill of being able to design a workable solution to the problem in the light of the realities they face.

Personal Characteristics of Managers

A manager, in addition to his professional abilities, must have certain personal characteristics, which are mentioned below:

1. *Intelligence:* A manager must have adequate intelligence to take quick decisions and to deal with problems. During certain critical situations they should use their intelligence for crisis management through spot decisions.
2. *Education:* Manager should also have the minimum required education in the particular profession as well as managerial education.

3. *Broad interest:* He must have broad interest to develop the organization to which he is heading.
4. *Desire to manage:* He must completely devote to the organization and he must take further interest to promote the enterprise.
5. *Ability to communicate:* He must be able to communicate freely and frankly with his superiors and subordinates.
6. *Integrity and honesty:* Managers have to deal with financial and other material resources and they should have integrity and honesty towards men and materials.
7. *Delegation:* Using the subordinates effectively, allocating decision-making and other responsibilities to the appropriate subordinates.
8. *Control:* Establishing procedures to monitor and regulate process, tasks or activities or subordinates and job activities and responsibilities; taking action to monitor the results of delegated assignments.
9. *Initiating:* Making attempts to influence events to achieve goals; self-starting rather than passive acceptance; taking actions to achieve goals beyond those called for.
10. *Tolerance:* Stability of performance under pressure or stress.
11. *Adaptability:* Maintaining effectiveness in varying environments with various tasks, responsibilities, or people.
12. *Tenacity:* Staying with a position or plan of action until the desired objective is achieved.

Types of Managers and their Tasks

Generally, in all organizations, the management level is divided into three, namely, lower management (first-line managers), middle management, and top management.

Lower management: The lower management (line-managers) direct non-management employees and they do not supervise other managers. Such lower level management managers are called as supervisors and foremen.

Middle management: Middle managers direct the activities of lower level managers. Their principal responsibilities are to direct the activities that implement their organizational policies and to balance the demands of their managers.

Top management: Top management is responsible for the overall management of an organization. These people are called as executives. They establish operating policies and guide the organization's growth and development. Top managers are also called by various names like chief executive officers (CEO), general manager, or manager. The top managers have to undertake liaison activities, monitoring activities, and the role of a negotiator.

With regard to the personal characteristics and skills needed, for various levels of managers, they vary from level to level. At the lower level management, technical skills are needed. Human skills are also needed here for the frequent interaction with the subordinates. At the middle management level, human skills are very essential and the conceptual skills gain importance. At the top management level, conceptual and design abilities and human skills are especially valuable.

Pre-Conditions for Developing Excellent Managers

1. *Willingness to learn:* Any manager must try to learn more. They must learn daily and they must learn from others' experiences.
2. *Acceleration of management development:* This denotes enriching the knowledge by means of attending seminars and conferences and through other means of knowledge.
3. *Importance of planning for innovation:* In the days of competition, the managers must be very particular about the future and they have to give importance for planning and innovations.
4. *Measuring and rewarding management:* One of the significant areas concerning the manager is importance of both objectively measuring managerial performance and of

rewarding good performance, imposing sanctions on a poor performance and providing corrective action wherever needed.

5. *Tailoring information:* This is to obtain the right information in the right form and at the right time. Tailoring information requires a high order of intelligence and design.
6. *Need for research and development in tools and techniques:* There exist a great need for research and development in management tools and techniques.
7. *Need for strong intellectual leadership:* Managing can no longer be only a practical art requiring merely native intelligence and experience. The rapid growth of knowledge warrants new thinking to provide new leadership.

Development Programmes Needed for Managers

As noted earlier, managers need new skills, knowledge and characteristics to manage their organizations. Some of such aspects are as follows:

1. *Decision-making skills:* This is an art, which can be developed by managers out of experience and interaction with other people. Decision-making skills can be enhanced through the use of management techniques like in-basket, business games, and case study.
2. *Interpersonal skills:* These skills can be developed through role playing, sensitivity training, transactional analysis, and structural insight.
3. *Job knowledge:* This can be enhanced through on-the-job experience, coaching, and understudies.
4. *Organizational knowledge:* This can be obtained through job rotation and multiple management.
5. *General knowledge:* Through special courses, meetings, and selective reading, general knowledge can be increased.
6. *Specific individual needs:* Through special projects and selected committee assignments, the individual needs could be satisfied.

Summary

- A manager is a key person and responsible for the day-to-day affairs and for the ultimate success of an organization. One way of understanding what manager do is to examine the functions of management.
- The managers require having technical, human, conceptual and designing skills.
- The managers are at different levels of management pyramid and perform different tasks.

Self-Learning Activity

Try to answer the following questions on your own:

1. Discuss the tasks performed by managers at various levels.
2. What type of development programmes are needed for managers?
3. List out the pre-conditions for developing excellent managers.

3

LEARNING

Learning is closely associated with training. Training and learning are inseparable and their ultimate goal is the same of inculcating new knowledge, skill, and techniques to the trainee. Learning implies a progressive change in individual's behaviour. It involves new ways of doing things and it operates an individual's attempt to overcome some barriers or to adjust themselves to new situations. Learning is the gathering of knowledge, attitude, habits, and skills. Learning is defined by Gate and others, "Learning may be thought of as the progressive change in behaviour, which is associated on the one hand with successive presentation of a situation, and on the other with repeated efforts of the individual to react to it effectively".

Characteristics of Learning

Yoakman and Simpson have enumerated nine general characteristics of learning, as follows:

1. *Learning is growth:* The word growth is generally associated with the body, which is growing, but through the mental growth of the learner. Learning is growth through experience.
2. *Learning is adjustment:* Learning helps an individual to adjust himself to the new situations. A new employee is

expected to learn new things by means of adjusting himself to new situations.

3. *Learning is organizing experience:* Learning is not mere addition to knowledge, but it is an organizing experience to a worker.
4. *Learning is purposeful:* Learning is based on certain specific purpose. According to Ryburn, 'this purpose is always connected with the use of some intrinsic power, with the use of the energy with which we are endowed with birth'. All work activities should be purposeful so that, a trainee should feel real urge for learning.
5. *Learning is intelligent:* Any work done mechanically is without any soul. Only efforts made intelligently have lasting effects.
6. *Learning is active:* Learning does not take place without a purpose and self-activity. In the learning process of a training, the activity of the trainee counts more than the activity of the trainer.
7. *Learning is both individual and social:* Learning is an individual activity and at the same time, more of a social activity. Individual mind is affected by the group mind because an individual is influenced by his friends, relatives, other trainees, etc. and learns their ideas, feelings, and notions. Social agencies have greater influence on the trainee and are always molding re-molding him.
8. *Learning is the product of environment:* Environment plays an important role in the growth and development of an individual. Environment should be healthy and rich in learning possibilities.
9. *Learning affects the conduct of the learner:* There is a change in the mental structure of a learner after every experience.

Principles of Learning

There are number of ways in which training can be made more effective by utilizing specific learning principles. The important principles of learning are described below:

1. *Motivation:* The best starting point is to state that trainees should want to learn. This is not to say that participation in a training programme without motivation would result in no learning. One principle that uses to make training interesting is to assure the active participation of the trainee. There are internal and external motivators. The internal motivators are within the individual. Competitive nature of training can serve as a good external motivator. The desire to do well is an important determinant of how much one receives out of a training programme.
2. *Reinforcement and feedback:* The principles of learning say that when one receives positive rewards or feelings for doing something, then it becomes more likely that one will do the same thing in similar situations. The trainer should attempt to increase the frequency of desirable behaviour through the correct use of various rewards. Rewards like prize, money, status, etc. will serve as reinforces. Feedback could make a training to correct his behaviour and makes the task more rewarding and stimulating.
3. *Practice and repetition:* The greater the opportunity to repeat or practice something when we learn, the better it is learned. With practice, individuals may become more familiar and at ease with what they are supposed to do. For certain managerial training courses, there could be multiple chances to play roles or practice behavioural skills. For other types of training involving motor skills, the trainee should be allowed to repeat the correct responses over and over.
4. *Meaningfulness of material:* The materials that are to be used in any training programme should be meaningful in the sense that it is understandable and interpretable by those participating in the training. It has been argued that training should be space out the learning periods rather than present them all together. When all the information is presented together, it seems to couple the

problems of not breaking the information down into smaller units. By spacing out the sessions, the material becomes easier to assimilate and practice.

5. *Transfer of training:* The purpose of training is to prepare an individual for some positions in the organization. One aspect of the training programme is therefore, the degree to which the material to be learned can be transferred to the job. The goal is to make the trainee's experience similar to the job experience. This can be done by making the training situation similar to the actual job situation in terms of the physical characteristics of the situation.
6. *Active involvement:* The trainee must take active involvement in the training and must make the training programme a productive one and successful one. As huge money is spent on training they should go waste.
7. *Individual approach:* In addition to the organization's initiative, the trainee must take individual care and attention to make the training programme a success.
8. *Feedback:* After the training is over, the organization and the training centers must get the opinions and reactions of the employees about the training programme.
9. *Evaluation:* All training programmes must end with the total evaluation from the angles of training institute, trainees and organization. A final evaluation alone can tell the utility of a training programme and the effectiveness of a training programme.

Methods of Making Learning Principles Applied to Training

1. *Trainee must be motivated to learn:* In order to learn, a person must want to learn. In the context of training, motivation influences a person's interest for training, keeps the attention focused on the training activities and re-enforces what is learned. Motivation is influenced by the belief and perceptions of the training. If the motivational factors are missing, a trainer may leave the training programme with nothing accomplished.

2. *Learning must be reinforced:* The learners learn best with immediate reinforcement of appropriate behaviour. The learner must be rewarded for new behaviour in ways that satisfy his need such as pay, recognition, and promotion. Standards of performance should be set for the learner. Benchmarks for learning will provide goals and gives a feeling of accomplishment when reached. These standards provide a measure for meaningful feedback.
3. *Trainer must provide for practice of the material:* Learning requires time to assimilate what has been learned, to accept it and to build confidence in what has been learned. This requires practice and repetition of the material.
4. *Material presented must be meaningful:* Appropriate materials for sequential learning (cases, problems, discussion outlines, etc.) must be provided. The trainer acts as aid in the learning process. The learning methods used should be varied. It is boredom that destroys learning, not fatigue.
5. *Material presented must be communicated effectively:* Any material given to the trainees must be presented properly. Communication must be done in a unified way with proper time to allow it to be absorbed.
6. *Material taught must transfer to the job situation:* The trainer must do his job best to make the training as close to the reality of the job as possible. When the trainee returns to his job, the training can be applied immediately.

Summary

- Learning is closely associated with training. Training and learning are inseparable and their ultimate goal is the same of inculcating new knowledge, skill, and techniques to the trainee. Learning implies a progressive change in individual's behaviour.
- There are learning principles and methods of making such principles applied to training.

Self-Learning Activity

Try to answer the following questions on your own:

1. What are the principles of learning?
2. Describe nine characteristics of learning.

4

Need for Training

Job Requirement

Every job requires certain characteristics and expected from an employee. They are as follows:

1. *Background knowledge:* Background knowledge of an employee relating to his educational background and experience background. This is needed to provide right job for the right man.
2. *Knowledge of application:* A job will require an employee the ability to apply this knowledge to job situations. Job situations vary and demand presence of mind and sense to take spot decisions.
3. *Tool subjects:* An employee, in addition to educational background and experience, must have additional knowledge on accounting, computer, statistics, etc. These are the days of competition and additional knowledge is required to improve the efficiency of working.
4. *Management techniques:* An employee in a management cadre is expected to know the minimum management techniques, like value analysis, ratio, PERT, etc. These tools help in decision-making process and save cost and time to the organization.

5. *Management skills:* Certain management skills cannot be taught, but they are learned through experience. Such skills are human relations, organizational behaviour, etc. A successful employee should acquire these skills to claim up the ladder of promotion fast.

Place of Training in Matching Man and his Job

In measuring the performance of an individual, he is given opportunities and his performance is evaluated through various tools. Training is one among such tools. Such tools are as follows:

1. *Performance appraisal:* Through periodical performance appraisals, an individual's job is measured. Performance appraisal is part of HRM and every organization frequently evaluate the performance of each employees.
2. *Performance review discussion and counseling:* It is a face-to-face review with the employee. The employee's strength and weakness are assessed at his face itself.
3. *Job rotation:* By means of shifting the job of an employee within the organization, his performance is measured. He is given different acts and experiences to perform.
4. *Organizational development activity:* By means of putting an employee under activities of MBO, corporate planning, etc we can measure his performance.
5. *Career development plan and activities:* Through individual career development plan, an employee's performance can be measured. He is expected to use all opportunities given to him.
6. *Training:* Training is an important measure through which an individual's job is matched to his abilities. Training is a continuous process in the career of an employee.

Relevance of Training

In the modern industrial and managerial context, training has the following relevance:

1. *Rapid changes in technology and production:* In the age of competition and technological changes, training is needed

to shape the employees. Every employee must make himself fit in the new technology and production methods.

2. *Handling of responsibilities different from their study specialization:* An employee may have a job unrelated to his basic education. To change him to the current situation, training is needed. There is vast gap between theory and practice. Training reduces this gap.
3. *Behavioural changes:* To have behavioural changes, an employee needs training. As an employee has to move with many people within the organization, behavioural changes are needed.
4. *Entry of backward and underprivileged in organization:* Sometimes, employees with local calibre may enter an organization. They have to match the efficiency of the peers. For them training has greater relevance.
5. *Mistakes in selecting wrong people:* Sometimes, organizations commit mistakes in selecting wrong people. Such people cannot be sent out and training can change them.
6. *College degree:* College degree can provide only theoretical knowledge. But skills, work situation, and needed experiences can be provided by training.

Importance/Objectives of Training

1. *To achieve a change in the behaviour of those trained:* An employee must be given training to change his negative behaviours and to serve the customers.
2. *To acquire new skills, technical knowledge, and problem-solving ability:* In a competitive world, lot of innovations are introduced in administration. The employees must acquire new skills and technical knowledge, which can be provided only by training.
3. *Training must be based on organizational and individual needs:* The training must take into consideration of the organizational needs and individual needs.

4. *Training should address problems:* When an organization faces problems, the training activities must address such problems and solutions found out.
5. *Training should be based on sound theories of learning:* Sound theories based on previous experiences must be taught to the trainees.
6. *Training must be evaluated:* Evaluation of training is a continuous process and each training must be evaluated to its effectiveness and modifications must be made.
7. *Organisations must face competition:* For the organizations, they must provide training to the employees to face competition in the market.
8. *Organisations must have customer attraction:* To attract more customers and to do service to the members, the employees must be given training.
9. *Organisations to update their service:* The service concept of Organisations is changing very often and to provide latest service, employees need training.

Benefits of Training

1. *Reduces learning time:* Training is learning by seeing. An employee is put under actual work situations and given training. This reduces the learning time.
2. *Improved performance:* Training can improve the present performance as well as future performance of an employee.
3. *Attitude formation:* Employees may have different perceptions about their job and their organization. They must be molded towards positive goals, thereby achieving the goals of the organization.
4. *Aid in solving problems:* Through training an employee can be taught about the problem-solving abilities.
5. *Fill manpower needs:* A growing organization may need experienced manpower for future purposes. Such manpower could be created through training.

6. *Benefits to employees:* Out of training an employee can learn new things, earn more, gets job security, and promotion.
7. *Greater delegation of authority:* Training can help an organization to delegate and decentralize power to the juniors.
8. *Creation of a reserve of qualified staff:* Every year employees retire from services and many may go out of a company. To replace such talents, trained staff can be kept as a reserve.
9. *Improved selection for promotion:* When promotion takes place, employees with training can be favored for such promotion.
10. *Minimum delay in staffing new positions:* When new positions are created in an organization, that place would be filled without any delay through trained employees.
11. *Improved executive morale:* Higher level executives must also be given training to improve their work culture and morale.
12. *Increased effectiveness and reduced cost resulting in greater profitability:* Training improves the quality of working through which wastage of time, energy and cost are reduced.

Place of Training for Cooperatives and other Organizations

1. *Training increases productivity:* Cooperatives and other organizations need to increase their productivity for their improved operational efficiency. Training can help.
2. *Improvement in employee morale:* Training improves the skills, confidence, and satisfaction, which develops new enthusiasm and pride of an employee.
3. *Availability for future personnel needs:* When cooperatives and other organizations grow, trained employees can occupy future higher posts.
4. *Improvement in health and safety of workers:* Proper training can prevent health and safety of workers in organizations.

5. *Reduced supervision:* Trained employees need not have any supervision over their work. This reduces overhead charge.
6. *Personal growth:* Training improves the personal talents and experiences of employees.
7. *Organizational stability:* Organisations can grow from strength to strength through trained people. They become asset to the organization.

Classification of Training

Types of training can be classified as follows:

1. *Interpersonal skills:* Leadership development, coaching, communication skills, team building, customer service, and other interpersonal skills.
2. *Technical:* Product training and knowledge, information technology, computer application, and other technical skills needed for a job.
3. *Business:* Finance, marketing, quality, strategic planning, organizational culture, etc.
4. *Mandatory:* Safety, health, sexual harassment, and other legal compliances.
5. *Performance management:* Training to improve the work performance.
6. *Problem solving/Decision-making:* Defining problems, creativity in developing alternatives, selecting solution.
7. *Personal:* Career planning, time management, personal finance, public speaking.

Training Trends and Key Training Issues

Training Trends

With the globalization of the economies, the economic trends in countries are changing fast. Manufacturing and services move towards mass production to meet a global market. The multinationals have taken the competition to the international arena. In this context, the importance of training has been recognised very much by the global players and national players.

Both economic and demographic trends suggest radical changes in the composition of the workforce of the 21st century. Other factors that affect the number, types, and requirement of available jobs include automation: continuing work displace as a function of mergers acquisition and downsizing; continuing and the shift from manufacturing to service jobs.

These issues suggest several reasons, why the time and money, budgeted for training, will increase during the next decades?

1. The number of unskilled and undereducated youth who will be needed for entry-level jobs, and the need to train currently underutilized groups of racial and ethnic minorities, women and older workers. This is the social challenge.
2. Increasingly sophisticated technological systems that will impose training and retraining requirements on the existing workforce. This is the high-performance work systems challenge.
3. Ongoing needs to meet the product and service needs of customers. This is the quality challenge.
4. The need, as more firms move to employee involvement and teams in the workplace, for team members to learn behaviours such as asking for ideas. Offering help without being asked, listening and feedback skills, and resigning and considering the ideas of others. This is the interpersonal challenge.

Training Issues

Johnson Controls programme illustrates some of the important training issues facing today's organizations. Specifically:

1. *Training to keep pace with a changing organizational environment*

   Johnson Controls confronts this challenge by taking an empowered approach to training in which teams of employees learn from each other. However, as equipment and techniques change, employees may have to receive training directed by managers (known as a top-down approach to training). Many organizations are turning to computerized options as an efficient means for delivering training. The computerized approach may not be the answer in all situations.

2. *Training to take place in a classroom setting or on the job*
   Classroom training may lack realism and not be as effective as training that occurs while on the job. However, on-the-job training can cause slowdowns that decrease production or irritate customers. Some originations use virtual reality (VR) technology to maximize the relevance of classroom training. However, this approach may not be applicable or cost-effective in other organizations.
3. *Training to be effectively delivered worldwide*
   Many of today's organizations conduct operations around the world. Consistent quality of products or service is critical to organizational survival in today's competitive markets. Johnson Controls' Team Rally event involves employees from around the world. Unfortunately achieving uniformity worldwide can be difficult. VR training provides solutions for companies that cannot afford VR training might include computer-teleconference or video based training.
4. *Is Training the solution?*
   A fundamental objective of training is the elimination or improvement of performance problems. However, not all performance problems call for training. Performance deficits can have several causes, many of which are beyond the worker, control and would therefore not be affected by training.

Before choosing training as the solution, management should carefully analyze the situation to determine if training is the appropriate response.

5. *Goals must be clear and realistic*

   To be successful, a training programme must have dearly stated and realistic goals. These goals will guide the programme's content and determine the criteria by which its effectiveness will be judged.

Unless the goal is clearly articulated before training programmes are set up, the organization is likely to find itself training employees for the wrong reasons and toward the wrong ends. For example, if the goal is to improve specific skills, the training needs to be targeted to those skill areas.

6. *Is the training a good investment?*

   In addition to the cost of delivering the training programme, there are costs associated with analyzing and evaluating the programme's effectiveness. In some cases training may be appropriate but not cost-effective. Before beginning a training programme, managers must weigh the cost of the current problem against the cost of training to eliminate it. It could be that the training cure is more costly than the performance ailment, in which case alternatives to training must be considered.

   Determining whether training is a good investment requires measuring the training's potential benefits in money. Training that focuses on "hard" areas (such as the running and adjustment of machines) that have a fairly direct impact on outcomes (such as productivity) can often be easily translated into a money value. Estimating the economic benefits of training in "softer" areas, such as teamwork and diversity training, is much more challenging.

7. *Will training work?*

   There are many types of training programmes in widespread use. Some types of training are more effective than others for some purposes and in some situations. Designing effective training remains as much an art as a science, however, because no single type of training has proved most effective overall.

Beyond the type of training and its content, a number of contextual issues can determine a training programme's effectiveness. For example, an organizational culture that supports change, learning and improvement can be a more important determinant of training programme's effectiveness than any aspect of the programme itself. Participants who view training solely as a day away from work are unlikely to benefit much from the experience. Furthermore, managers do not endorse the content and purpose of the training, it is unlikely that the training programme will have any influence on work processes.

Structural Issues in Training

Certain structural issues must be addressed if training systems are to reach their full potential. Here are some problems often identified at the macro level.

1. *Corporate commitment is lacking and uneven*

   Most companies spend nothing at all on training. Those that do tend to concentrate on managers, technicians, and professionals, not rank-and-file workers. This is changing, as a result of the rapid pace of introduction of new technology, combined with new approaches to organization design and production management, many companies simply cannot afford to overlook training. Workers have to learn three kinds of new skills:

   (a) Ability to use the new technology.

   (b) Ability to maintain it.

   (c) Ability to diagnose system problems.

   In an increasingly competitive marketplace, the ability to implement rapid changes in products and technologies is often a key requirement to preserve the competitive edge.

2. *Expenditures on training are inadequate*

   The American Society for Training and Development urges business to increase training expenditures to at least 2 per cent of their annual payrolls on training-up from the current U.S. industry average of 1.2 per cent. Leading companies invest much more: General Electric (4.6) per cent of payroll) U.S Robotics (4.2%) Motorola (4%) Texas instruments (3%).

3. *There is no guarantee that graduates have mastered skills*
As a result, business must spend large amounts of money to retrain workers in basic skills. In a recent survey, companies reported that on average, 34.1 per cent of applicants lack functional workplace literacy—the ability to read instructions, write reports, or do arithmetic at a level adequate to perform common workplace tasks. However only about 6.5 per cent of the companies provide remedial training in these basic skills.

4. *Poaching trained workers*
It is a major problem for US businesses, and provides a strong disincentive for training. Unlike Germany where local business groups pressure companies not to steal each other's employees, there is no such system in countries like United States. Despite this problem business may have no choice but to train. As Gary Token, CEO of Motorola, says, "If knowledge is becoming antiquated at a faster rate, we have no choice but to spend on education".

5. *Training being viewed as an investment*
Current accounting rules require that it be treated as an expense. Business might spend more on training if accounting rules were revised. Unlike investments in plant and expenditures, when show on books as asset, training expenses are seen merely as expenditures to be deducted in the year in which they are incurred.

6. *Government is not providing enough funds as for retraining to help workers displaced*
Throughout the industrialized world government leaders are focusing on one of the most corrosive dangerous trends of the new millennium: the inability of modern economies to ease the transitions that the young, the poor and older workers must make to keep up with rapid technological changes in the workplace.

7. *Closer ties between employers and schools*
   Close relationship is needed between the companies and the business schools. At present in many parts of the world such collaboration is lacking, resulting in poor quality of training.

Limitations of Training

1. *Time and energy needed to plan and analyze results:* Training needs lot of time and planning. So, an organization must keep this factor in mind. Separate establishment and budget are needed to make training effective and productive.
2. *Coordination of different managers:* The success of training depends on the coordination of various managers in an organization. Managers committed to their departments may have loyalties to their departments. To work for a common goal training acts as a unifying force.
3. *Subjective evaluation:* Training evaluation must be made objectively. But in certain cases subjective evaluation takes place due to human error.
4. *It should be continuous process:* Training should be a continuous process and should not be made a stop gap arrangement. Majority of the organizations forget this fact and make training as an important input.
5. *Full preparation and planning:* To make a training programme successful, planning and preparation are needed before and after the training. Full time organizational arrangement is needed. In many organizations it is part of some other department.
6. *Evaluation:* Every training should end with evaluation. An evaluation should be impartial and productive. Many organizations skip evaluation due to lack of qualified manpower.
7. *Quality of training:* Quality of training is decided by cost, and energy spent by an organization. So, an organization would be ready to spend money on it.

8. *Seriousness of training by employees:* The employees must take training as a serious matter. They should not take it as a paid vacation. It is a universal lesson that training is not taken seriously by concerned parties.
9. *Alternative arrangement for training period:* Whenever an employee undergoes training, alternative arrangement for his work must be arranged.
10. *Training should be innovative:* The training programme must be conducted by experienced training centers and the training programme should be innovative and not repetitive.

Summary

- Needs, objectives, benefits of training are discussed in this chapter.
- Different tools for measuring the performance of individuals in organizations, training trends and training issues are also discussed.

Self-Learning Activity

Try to answer the following questions on your own:

1. What are the tools for measuring the performance of employees in organizations?
2. List out benefits of training.
3. Give an account of training issues.

5

LEVELS OF TRAINING

VARIOUS LEVELS OF OFFICIALS

Officials are executives of cooperative organizations and other organizations can be classified as: top management, middle management, and lower management.

1. *Top Management:* Top management consists of higher levels officials of an organization. Such officials are managers, general managers, heads of various departments like production, marketing, materials, finance, personnel, etc. Such executives are involved in organizational planning, execution, monitoring, evaluation, and budgeting. They will also be engaged in training the lower level staff. They move vary closely with the organization and they act as eyes and ears of the organization.

2. *Middle Management:* Staff here usually consists of middle aged executives who are either recruited directly or promoted from the lower level. Such staff are deputy managers, accountants, and in charges of various sub-sections. They act as balancing force between lower level management and higher level management. Based on their performance, these officials will be promoted at stages. In big companies, which have branches, these officials may be transferred from one place to another place.

3. *Lower Management:* Staff coming under this category have to be guided by middle management officials or top management officials. Such staff will have lower educational qualifications and may not be exposed to training and development. They are paid poorly and such staffs are workers in factories, menial staff, and clerical staff.

SUITABILITY OF TRAINING AT VARIOUS LEVELS

Training has greater relevance to the organization, the individual, and the society. The method of training, the cost and the content must have utility to all. Otherwise, training for the sake of training will defeat the purpose of training and the money and time spent on training will go waste. The suitability of training is discussed as under:

1. **Organization**

   Training has greater relevance and suitability to the organization because it has to increase its performance, profit, and operational efficiency. To achieve the corporate goals of the organization, training has greater suitability at all levels. In the case of cooperatives, training is an in-built system and employees at all levels are expected to undergo training. Cooperatives have established training centers at various levels on a permanent basis.

2. **Activity**

   This denotes the particular or the special aspects of training. Training is a broader term and it must have relevance to the institution, individual, and above all it should be activity-based. Various activities can be grouped under production, materials, finance, marketing, personnel, etc. For cooperatives, the focus can be on member satisfaction measures and increasing the operational efficiency.

3. **Individual**

   The suitability of training must have the relevance to the taste, preference, and aptitude of the individual. The particular individual who is selected for training must view the training perspective more seriously and productively. Money spent on training is a scare resource and should not go waste because of the negative attitude or indifference of the employee towards training. He must willingly take the programme seriously and make the training useful to the organization and to himself. The individual employ's personal attitude must coincide with the objectives and philosophies of the organization.

4. **Period of training**

   Training programmes are arranged for various durations ranging from short term, medium term, and long term. Even capsule programmes for a very short period are conducted by training centers. It is up to the individual and the organization to decide the period of training. Other factors involved in choosing the period of training are cost, time, place of training, training organizer, etc.

5. **On-the-job training**

   This is the widely used method of training, which means putting the worker on the job under the close supervision of a trained worker and of training aids and techniques such as lectures, role play, etc. If it is not handled properly the cost can be high in damaging machinery, unsatisfied customers, and poorly taught workers. To prevent these problems, trainers must be carefully selected and trained. The trainee should be placed with a trainer who is similar in background and personality. The trainer should be motivated by training and rewarded for doing it well.

One approach to systematic on-the-job training is Job Instruction Training (JIT) system developed during World War II. In this system, the trainers first train the supervisors, who in turn train the other employees.

Job Instruction Training (JIT) methods

Step 1 *Ready to teach the job*

- *(a)* Under this step, things must be decided to do the job efficiently, safely, economically, and intelligently.
- *(b)* The trainee must be provided with proper tools, equipments, supplies, and materials.

(c) The workplace must be properly arranged to keep good work atmosphere.

Step 2 Preparation of the learner

(a) Put the learner at ease.

(b) Find out what he knows already about the job.

(c) Get the learner interested in learning the job.

Step 3 Presentation of the operations and knowledge

(a) Tell, show, illustrate, and question about new knowledge and operations.

(b) Instruct slowly, clearly, completely, and patiently one point at a time.

(c) Check, question, and repeat.

(d) Make sure the learner really knows.

Step 4 Performance tryout

(a) Test the learner by having him perform the job.

(b) Ask questions beginning with why, how, when, and where.

(c) Observe performance, correct errors, and repeat instructions.

(d) Continue until you know the learner knows.

Step 5 Follow up

(a) Put the employee "on his own".

(b) Check frequently to be sure that learner follows instructions.

(c) Make close follow-up until the person is qualified to work with normal supervision.

Methods followed under on-the-job training

(a) *Coaching and counseling:* Under this method, a senior manager gives continued coaching and counseling to a new manager. He should answer all questions and explain why things are done in such ways. It is the duty of the manager-trainee to view that he learned everything and performed adequately.

(b) *Transfers and rotations:* By means of transferring an employee from one job to another, new type training can be given under the supervision of an experienced manager.

(c) *Apprenticeship programme:* Under this system, an employee is put under training for few years. During this period the trainee is paid less than a fully qualified worker. He is given careful training under an experienced master worker.

(d) *Job instruction training:* This method is basically, based on instructions being given to the new workers. By means of using job instructions, a trainee can achieve good results.

(e) *Creation of assistant-to positions:* Such positions are created to broaden the view of the trainees by allowing them to work closely with experienced managers who can give special attention to the developmental needs of trainees. The managers give selected assignments to test the judgment of the trainees.

(f) *Temporary promotions:* Temporary promotions are given to the employees and they are given training by the senior managers. If they perform well they are retained in the promotion.

(g) *Committees and junior boards:* Under this system, trainees are given opportunities to interact with experienced managers. They come across with variety of issues concerning the organization. They create good relationship with different departments. Trainees will also be given opportunity to submit reports and proposals to the committees.

6. **Off-the-job training**

Off-the-job training is conducted in a classroom with on-the-job situation to work with. Many organizations prefer this method since it does not disrupt the normal working. Various methods of the off-the-job training are as follows:

(a) *Conference/Discussion approach:* Under this method, the trainee is brought under classroom situation and he is expected to participate in discussions. The lectures are supplemented with audio-visual aids such as blackboards, etc. These lectures are video taped or audio taped.

(b) *Programmed instruction and computer assisted instruction:* Under this method, materials are prepared on teaching machines or in text form and learning principles are followed. Under this system, instruction is given without the presence or intervention of a human instructor. The learner learns at his own rate. The instruction is presented in small steps requiring frequent responses by the learner.

(c) *Simulation exercises:* It is a method under which a trainee is put under artificial environment that closely initiates working conditions. Simulation activities include case exercises, experimental exercise, computer-based training, etc.

(d) *Case studies:* Case studies present an in-depth description of a particular problem an employee might come across in his job. The employee attempts to find and analyze the problem, evaluates alternative courses of action, and decides the right course.

(e) *Vestibule training:* Under this system, employees learn their jobs on the equipment they will be using, but the training is conducted away from the workplace.

QUALITY OF TRAINING AT VARIOUS LEVELS

Quality of training in general depends on the following factors:

1. *Commitment to the goals of the organization:* If an organization is committed to its goals, it will have faith in using the training for its employees. It will be ready to invest in its staff and training. This will improve the quality of training.

2. *Training environment:* This refers to the physical infrastructure required like classrooms, library, hostels, etc as well as sitting arrangements, layout of the classrooms, teaching aids, and recreational facilities.
3. *Professionalism of the trainers:* The trainers must be well experienced in the fields of their choice and must have exposed to various situations. Their experiences should be bread-based and they must be ready to help all trainees to understand each ones capacity to receive the training.
4. *Adequacy of funds and resources:* This is relating to the training centers. They must have enough resources to provide infrastructure, good salary to the staff, and comforts to the trainees.

Quality of training at top management

To give quality of training at the top level the following factors must be considered:

1. *Computer-oriented:* Training for top management must be computer-oriented and it must be linked to internet, e-commerce, etc.
2. *Latest information:* The training centers must impart the latest techniques and information to the trainees. Such techniques must be related to the topics of training.
3. *Concern over competitors' ability:* Employees are given training to equip themselves qualitatively to meet the competitors' ability.
4. *Personal comforts:* The personal comforts of the trainees like travel arrangements, food, secretarial assistance, etc must be given care.
5. *Using latest teaching techniques:* The trainees must be taught latest management games and latest teaching techniques.
6. *Mutual exchange of information:* The trainees must be given opportunity to share the experience of others, so that they can learn new things from others.
7. *Appraisal/Evaluation:* All training programmes must be evaluated to measure the efficiency of the training

programme. Appraisal standards must be fixed to evaluate top management trainee.

Quality of training at middle management

1. *Computer-oriented:* Like the top management, these people must also be given computer-oriented training.
2. *Issue related discussions:* The discussions during the training period must be based on issues common to all trainees.
3. *Visit to similar institutions:* During the training period, the trainees must be taken to institutions similar to them.
4. *Training accountability:* Every trainee must fully utilize the training and must practice its utility in their institutions once the training is over.
5. *Appraisal/Evaluation:* At the end of the training programme, each training must be evaluated on his performance and usefulness of the training.

Quality of training at lower level

1. *Nearer location:* To make the training effective for the lower level employees, the training place must be nearer to them.
2. *Light syllabus:* The training curriculum should be light to such people as they have low level of education.
3. *More exposure visits:* More visits to institutions can be arranged.
4. *Evaluation:* Training evaluation must be made at the end of the training programme. Those who undergone training must be made accountable by increased work performance.

Summary

- Officials are executives of cooperative organizations and other organizations can be classified as: top management, middle management, and lower management.
- Training has greater relevance to the organization, the individual, and the society. The method of training, the cost and the content must have utility to all. The quality must be maintained at all levels of training.

Self-Learning Activity

Try to answer the following questions on your own:

1. Describe on-the-job training.
2. What are the factors to be considered to maintain quality of training at top level?

6

Training Process

Training process means the day-to-day activities relating to training that make up the annual training cycle. Concentrating on the process is the best place for improving the training efficiency. Effective training has to be aligned with a company's business directions and values, that the training department has to provide courses, which support company's goals, and that anyone who is involved in managing the training process has to have a clear idea of where the business is going. This means that for effective training the business basics of the company should also be cared for.

Business Basics of an Organization

1. *Alignment:* The key to getting the basics right is making sure that everyone has the same understanding of the current situation and that everyone is moving towards that direction for the future. Without alignment no company can make progress and no training department can provide effective training.
2. *Philosophy:* A philosophy is a statement of what the company stands for. It is a set of values and beliefs by which actions can be judged. A philosophy makes it clear of which behaviours are appropriate and which are not unacceptable.

3. *Mission:* A mission is a statement of what a company has to do. A mission should describe—what is done for whom in such a way that it cannot be confused with any others' mission.
4. *Assessment:* Assessment is very much about the understanding of where the company is today, and determining the reasons for both success and failure.
5. *Vision:* A vision is a picture where the organization wants to be in future. By describing the future, a vision can exert a strong pulling force, which helps keep the organization aligned.
6. *Goals:* Goals are quantitative figures such as sales, profit, and market share. Without goals, the vision will remain a dream.
7. *Policies:* A policy is a medium to long-range course of action comprising a goal and a strategy. A strategy is the means of achieving a goal.
8. *Policy deployment:* It is a process of ensuring that the company's policies for quality, cost, and delivery are understood throughout the company. Policy deployment is a cyclical process. Progress against goals should be checked, the reasons for any deviation diagnosed and the policies modified in the light of the diagnosis.

Company's Attitude Towards Training

In a company from top management to the lower management, a right attitude should be set towards training, its objectives, utility, and cost effectiveness. The training department has to get its own house in order and the organization has to be aware of the importance that is attached to training. Training has to be aligned with the business directions of the company. The training function should in no doubt as to which business direction and values should be supported. Where there is risk of fragmentation or misalignment of the training effort, it is vital that all the key players within the training community agree on the following areas:

(a) *Training mission:* Where there is more than one training organization within a company, it becomes imperative that the coverage provided by each training department is understood and well defined. They should make it clear as to what type of training is provided for which type of workers.

(b) *Training philosophy:* Training philosophy is a statement of a company's attitude towards training. It has to define clearly the importance that is attached to training. It has to be communicated to every employee.

(c) *Training policy:* In the same way that a business policy has a goal and the means to attain the goal, a training policy should also have targets and measures. The managers have to provide the means for releasing new employees for training.

(d) *Training standards:* The training standards are such as:

  (i) hours of training per employee;

  (ii) additional hours of training for managers;

  (iii) minimum level of training before starting a new job;

  (iv) the amount and timing of the induction training.

The following are some of the standards set for training:

- trainer to student ratio
- trainer trainee
- trainer accreditation
- cost per trainee-day
- cost per trainer-day
- classroom standards
- administrative standards
- course development standards

Responsibility for Training

It is important to consider who is to be responsible for training, and who will deliver training.

Training departments

From the 1950s and (particularly) the 1960s, the responsibility for and delivery of training in many large organizations rested very much with specialist departments. By the 1980s and 1990s, however, training departments had come in for considerable criticism. They were accused of:

- being too rigid to respond to the changing needs of the organization;
- being too much of an administrative expense;
- having lost contact with the changing skills needed on the shop floor or at the place of work;
- being self-serving and bureaucratic;
- providing training that was too theoretical and not sufficiently practically based;
- not providing training and development that met individual needs-courses were too class/group based.

Despite these criticisms, training departments remain important in many organizations because they have personnel who have specialized knowledge and skills in the provision of training. As HRD becomes more important in the organization the role of providers is becoming increasingly pivotal as facilitators of learning and the exchange of information and knowledge. The concepts of the learning organization and the knowledge-based organization place learning and HRD at the very heart of the organization. HRD departments also act as internal consultants giving support to line managers alongside the HR department.

Training consultancies

Over the past decade the number of consultancies, many of them specializing in training, has become an industry. While there are many excellent consultancies, there are also the inevitable operations, which sometimes have unqualified, inexperienced and untrained staff, and at present there is no regulation to stop such operations from being set up.

It would be naïve to believe that consultants are brought into organizations only to provide training programmes. They are also used to resolve political conflicts, to justify having larger budgets, to support political maneuvering, and for other questionable reasons.

Training and the line manager

In order to counteract the perceived inflexibilities of training and personnel departments, there has been a notable trend to devolve many functions to line managers, including training policy. The justification is usually couched in terms of meeting the needs of people, where it matters, at workplace level. Part of the line manager's brief it to discern the training needs of individuals in their department, and to suggest suitable training for them, usually in consolation with the personnel or training department. Training budgets have increasingly been devolved to line managers, in the belief that funding can be spent most effectively at the point where needs have been identified.

This can be very effective because the assessment and delivery of training is more closely attuned to people in their working environment, but its efficacy depends very much on how it is carried out.

Training Process

1. *Accountability and responsibility:* In the case of training an executive must take accountability and responsibility for training. It is the training manager who has to make sure that nothing goes wrong between the steps of training process.
2. *Identifying the stakeholders:* A stakeholder is a person who has a vested interest in the outcome of the process. Managers, heads of departments, and workers are all the stakeholders in the training process.
3. *Defining and documenting the training process:* Definition of a process involves establishing a beginning and end points of a process. The following guidelines will help to decide the boundaries.

(a) The beginning of the process is where one takes control over from someone else.

(b) The end of the process is where one hands over the control to the other.

Brief Overview of Steps of Training Process

1. *Identify needs:* The process starts by identifying the business needs and turning these needs into training requirements.
2. *Evaluate needs:* The training needs must be evaluated by the concerned people.
3. *Select courses:* The choice will be between using an existing course, buying an external course and developing new course.
4. *Develop courses:* If no suitable courses are available, new courses have to be developed.
5. *Determine workload:* Here we have to decide the resources needed to meet the training.
6. *Select trainers:* Before the course is delivered suitable trainers must be identified and selected.
7. *Develop trainers:* The trainers must be given training.
8. *Certify trainers:* If a course is new to the trainers they should undergo programme of observation and practice to ensure that they reach the required standard before they are allowed to handle a training programme.
9. *Identify location and resources:* The place of training and the resources needed should be identified.
10. *Finalize the budget:* The budget needed for the training must be finalized.
11. *Finalize the training plan:* While finalizing the training plan, priority should be given for courses, trainees, and place.
12. *Pre-course administration:* Once the training plan has been agreed, then we have to ensure that identified people get to the right course at the right time.

13. *Prepare the course:* Before the courses can be delivered, the trainers need to prepare themselves, the materials, and the training rooms. The trainees must also prepare themselves for the course.
14. *Deliver the course:* Course delivery is the culmination of all efforts and it is the starting point of the change process in training.
15. *Validate training:* Validation is the process of ensuring that the course meets and continues to meet its stated objectives. Tests, observations, and feedback are all the data that have to be analyzed to determine whether the objectives are being met.
16. *Post-course administration:* As soon as the training has been completed, attendance on the course should be noted on the trainees' records.
17. *Transfer learning:* The trainees have to use the knowledge and the skills to ensure that learning is transferred into the business.
18. *Evaluate training:* Any training programme should be evaluated.
19. *Revise courses:* The courses then need to be revised to incorporate the changes identified during evaluation.

Checkpoints of Training Process

The major checkpoints of the training process are as follows:

1. Needs analysis and evaluation
2. Pilot courses (within course development)
3. Trainer certification
4. Finalize budget
5. Finalize training plan
6. Course preparation
7. Validate training
8. Evaluation

Summary

- Training process means the day-to-day activities relating to training that make up the annual training cycle. Concentrating on the process is the best place for improving the training efficiency.
- In a company from top management to the lower management, a right attitude should be set towards training, its objectives, utility, and cost effectiveness.

Self-Learning Activity

Try to answer the following questions on your own:

1. Write short notes on: Training Standards.
2. Discuss about training process.
3. What are the check points of training process?

7

Objectives of Training

An objective is a statement describing the knowledge or skills that the trainee is to acquire as a result of training. Setting training objectives helps to pinpoint exactly where we are going. The objectives of training provide the following:

1. A record of conditions that existed prior to the training.
2. A basis for evaluation of the training.

There are two approaches relating to the objectives of training, namely Reactive approach and Pro-active approach.

Reactive approach is a process, which takes into account the immediate needs related to organization's problems. This is more towards equipping the individual to solve organizational problems.

Pro-Active approach is based on long term plan of the organization taking into account the future needs.

Steps in Setting the Objectives

1. Write down the nature of the job or task for which training is to be done.
2. Include the quality standard that is to be attained through training.
3. Include the quantity standard that must be attained through training.

4. Add to the objectives any procedures and equipment criteria that are needed.
5. Alter the objectives as required to provide time for learning.
6. Review the objectives based on the realistic approach of the employees.
7. Gauge whether or not the desired amount of improvement can be attained through training.

   What Training is not

   (a) It is not an excuse for providing employees with a break in their work routine.

   (b) It is not a way to recognize or to praise good performance.

   (c) It is not a part of a reward or incentive system.

Relevance of Training to Various Areas

Training has relevance to the following four areas:

1. ***New employees***

   New employees must be given training and training objectives must be framed for them. So, decide the number of employees entering into the organization. Decide the number of employees who will be transferred from one department to other.

2. ***Performance improvement***

   To improve the performance of the present employees, training is needed and training objectives must be suitably framed.

3. ***Operational problems***

   To face operational problems in organizations, training is essential and training objectives must be framed. If the problem is related to training, it can be tackled through training. There are certain indicators to show the operational problems.

   (a) Continuing mistakes and errors in the job.

   (b) Excessive time needed to do the work.

(c) Employees requesting transfers.
(d) Performance is low or decreasing.
(e) Employees are reluctant to take new responsibilities.

4. ***Employee development***

Employee development denotes the development of the employees for future purposes. Training should match the development of employees. While the employee development is designed, it can be noted that all high performers must be given some sort of training. Training should not be dumped on them, which may affect their growth. It should help to improve the productivity of the organization and improve the skills in the areas of communication, leadership, and inter-personal relationship.

Objectives of Training to Organizations

1. *Training should address problems that need solutions:* An organization must have number of weapons to solve the problems faced by it. One such tool is training. So, training must be related to the solving of the problems directly by the employees who undergo training.
2. *It should ensure that resources reach the right priorities:* Resources spent on training must be used more productively. It should not go waste and the results should ensure the worth of the money spent on training.
3. *To provide a central plank in any development plan:* All right thinking organizations give greater importance to training in their development plan. Investment on training is investment on human beings, which is very essential to improve the quality of working.
4. *It must be result-oriented:* As considerable amount of budget is meant for training in organizations, it must produce the expected results to the organizations. The expected results of training are quality in working, quickness of service, saving of cost, reducing the time span of work, and a forecast on the future of the organization.

5. *It must provide cost-effective solutions:* When the money spent on training is huge the results of such training cannot be measured quantitatively. On the other hand it should result in quick services and satisfaction to the trainee, organization, training center, and the customers of the particular organization.
6. *It must ensure a positive return to the investment:* As already stated, the return on the investment of training cannot be measured quantitatively. It should result in qualitative return to the investment made by the organization.
7. *It must be a continuous process:* Training should be made a continuous process. It should be made an obligation to all types of employees. Every year, organizations must allocate funds for training.

Objectives of Training to Individuals

1. *It must improve the skill, knowledge, and understanding of the individual:* Training must impart new skills to the individual, which can motivate him to do more work skillfully. It must also increase the knowledge, wisdom, personality, and understanding of the individual.
2. *It must increase the individual's values:* Values like loyalty, faithfulness to duty, selfless service, commitment to the organization, etc must be nursed and cultivated by any training programme.
3. *A new enthusiasm to work with others:* The trainee must expand the wisdom and knowledge of employees and must lead the employee to work with others. Such team spirit will be an asset to the organization and this will enhance the abilities of the individual.
4. *It should act as a motivator:* One of the non-monetary motivators to an individual is the job satisfaction and job enrichment. Training gives both of these satisfactions to an employee.
5. Improvement in the quality of working after training. Every training programme should have short-term and

long-term objectives. Such objectives must improve the quality of the work of employees after training.

6. *Prepare the individual for new tasks and responsibilities:* Organizations select individuals to undergo training, forecasting certain expectations from the individuals and the training. Without the knowledge of the employees, the organizations may make them ready for new responsibilities such as to head a new branch, to open a new office, prepare indexes for competition, etc.
7. *It must improve ones' human relations:* The ultimate objective of training to individual is to improve the human relations. It implies improvement in human relations than it was existing during previous occasions.

Steps to Effective Training

1. *Identification and integration of training needs or discover the training needs*

   An organization must identify the training needs of the employees at frequent intervals; rather a separate mechanism should be introduced by an organization in identifying the training needs. Inter-department assessment of training needs and prioritizing the training needs must be framed. Such identification of training must be integrated with the problems of the organization so that the problems could be tackled by training.
2. *Identify problems or gaps between the actual and expected levels of activities*

   In any activity of the organization, there will found to arise gap between the actual performance and expected performance. Training must fill such gaps and try to solve the problems of the organization through the employees and their training.
3. *Device monitoring techniques*

   Training programmes introduced must be monitored scientifically, so that it will give good results to the individual as well as the organization. Monitoring techniques can be developed on the following lines:

(a) *Variance analysis:* This technique is used for monitoring budgets and identification of training needs. Any deviation from the budget is noted and corrected then-and-there.

(b) *Asking questions:* Through this technique, the employees who had undergone training will be administered questions randomly. This is a type of survey and this technique has wider application in organizations.

4. *View the unexpected problems with an open mind*

   Any organization has to face risks and unexpected problems in its day to day operations. The employees and the organization must be ready to face such problems with an open mind, so that routine works will not be disturbed. Training can be helpful on such occasions.

5. *Identify the individuals and activities*

   In any organization, an individual is secondary to the organization. Organization is greater that individual. Training will become effective only when the ultimate objective of training results in organization development.

6. *Plan and take appropriate action to meet the training needs*

   While imparting training, the training needs of the organization like the type of training to be given, time to be sent for training, the training institution, place of training, budget for training, and training evaluation must be planned properly.

Summary

- An objective is a statement describing the knowledge or skills that the trainee is to acquire as a result of training. Setting training objectives helps to pinpoint exactly where we are going.
- There are two approaches relating to the objectives of training, namely Reactive approach and Pro-active approach.

Self-Learning Activity

Try to answer the following questions on your own:

1. Give an account of steps in setting training objectives.
2. What are the objectives of training to individuals?

8

TRAINING NEEDS ASSESSMENT

Meaning

It is a rational way of deciding what kind of training activity to undertake, to make an analysis of the entire organization (people, job technology, etc) and to identify trouble spots where training may help. So it is to decide:

(a) what kind of training is needed;

(b) to identify trouble spots where training may help;

(c) it can identify the shortcomings of the organization and help to reduce or master these shortcomings;

(d) training needs assessment must continue on a regular basis.

The training need can arise at any of the three levels: the organization, the activity, and the individual.

Objectives

1. *To ensure that resources reach the right priorities:* An organization may have to spend its resources on various items for which priorities must be evolved. Priorities like short-term training or long-term training, to send the lower level official or higher level official, to send the staff for training at the nearer center or far away place, etc.

2. *To help the central plan of the organization:* An organization may have to allocate money in its budget for various expenditures ranging from materials purchase, payment of wages, promotion and advertisement, etc. A training needs assessment plan can help the organization to plan their central plan properly and give importance to training.
3. *It enhances the progress of the organization towards investors and people:* Investment on human beings in the form of training will not go waste. On the other hand, it will have more productivity on the work as well as it can increase the individual's efficiency and integrity to the organization. So, training needs assessment is necessary.
4. *To help individuals and groups perform better, making positive contribution to job satisfaction, morale, and motivation:* The training needs assessment can help individuals and groups to perform their activities to their respective satisfaction and to achieve the common goals of the organization. Upon the individuals it can provide job satisfaction, which is an essential element for the growth of the personality of an individual worker. It can also uplift the morale of the employees and can act as motivator to do more work.
5. *Being a natural system of appraisal system, it encourages discussions on what skills need to be improved:* When assessment is made about training lot of discussions, reviews, and exchange of information must continue. Such functions will make the training needs assessment more effective and productive.
6. *To provide a constructive basis for enhancing performance and efficiency:* Any training programme should result in improved performance and efficiency on the part of the individual workers. A training assessment can certainly provide a constructive basis for the entire programme.
7. *To predict future job preference:* After the training is over an employee may be given an option by the organization to take up new jobs or additional assignments. Any training

needs assessment programme can predict quite earlier the future job preference of individual employees sent for training.

8. *To provide a clear and logic acceptable to participants:* A training assessment programme can be made step-by-step evaluation and assessment of training programmes. Between one area of training programme and another area of training programme a link or continuity should be given. This logic of training is made perfect by training needs assessment programme.
9. *To enhance the image of the company/cooperatives:* As training used to become a continuous process in organizations and cooperatives, the training needs assessment programme will naturally enhance the image of the organization in the minds of the share-holders, investors, public, government, and even on competitors.
10. *To provide equal opportunity to all employees:* Through training needs assessment programme an organization can assess the merits and demerits of individual employees and based on such evaluation equal opportunity could be given to all individuals based on priority.
11. *To supplement the organizations process for human resources development (HRD):* Human Resources Development is a significant area in an organization, which is the brain center of that organization. Numbers of activities like selection, interview, induction, training, promotion, welfare measures, etc are undertaken. To make all these functions of HRD more effective training needs assessment is very essential.

Levels of Analysis

There are three levels of analysis for determining the needs that training can fulfill:

(a) Organization analysis

(b) Operations analysis

(c) Individual analysis

Organizational analysis: It focuses on identifying where within the organization training is needed. At a general level, it is important to analyze training needs against the backdrop of organizational objectives and strategies. Unless you do this, you may waste time and money on training programmes that do not advance the cause of the company. Preemployment training programmes (PET) are prime examples of close alignment between organizational needs and training curricular. PET programmes are industry-specific, community-based coalitions. Member companies contribute time, money, and expertise to design training. And they also contribute employees to teach courses.

It is essential to analyze the organization's external environment and internal climate. Trends in the strategic priorities of a business, judicial decisions, civil rights laws, union activity, accidents, turnover, absenteeism, and on-the-job employee behaviour will provide relevant information at this level.

In summary, the critical first step is to relate training needs to the achievement of organizational goals. If you cannot make that connection, the training is probably unnecessary. However, if training need does surface at the organizational level. An operations analysis is the next step.

Operations Analysis

Operations analysis attempts to identify the content of training — what an employee must do in order to perform competently. It requires a careful examination of the work to be performed after training. It involves:

1. a systematic collection of information that describes how work is done, so that standards of performance for that work can be determined;
2. how tasks are to be performed to meet the standards; and
3. the competencies necessary for effective task performance.

Job analyses, performance appraisal, interviews (with jobholders, supervisors, and higher management), and analyses of operating problems (quality control, downtime reports, and customer complaints) all provide important inputs to the analysis of training needs.

Individual Analysis

Finally, there is individual analysis. It determines how well each employee is performing the tasks that make up his or her job. At this level, training needs may be defined in terms of the following general idea: The difference between desired performance and actual performance is the individual's training need. Performance standards, identified in the operations analysis phase, constitute desired performance. Each employee's actual performance can be compared to standards that represent desired performance by using information such as the following: Individual performance data; diagnostic ratings of employees by their supervisor's peers, or customers; records of performance kept by workers in diary form; attitude surveys; interviews; or tests (job knowledge, work sample, or situational). A gap between actual and desired performance may be filled by training.

However, assessing the needs for training does not end here. To evaluate the results of training and to assess what training is needed in the future, it is important to analyze needs regularly and at all three levels:

- At the organizational level, senior managers who set the organization's goals should analyze needs.
- At the operations level, the managers (or teams) who specify how the organization's goals are going to be achieved should analyze needs.
- At the individual level, the managers and workers who do the work to achieve those goals should analyze needs, keeping in mind that performance is a function both of ability (hence, training) and motivation (a worker who wants to perform well.)

Causes which warrants training

The most frequent causes of poor performance in workplace, which warrants training usually involve one or more of these factors:

1. *Lack of skills:* Either employees never knew how to do their jobs properly, or they forget. If a former typist is not as productive after switching to a word processor, the problem could be that the person does not know how to use the new system effectively. Fortunately, this is usually the type of problem most readily solved through training.
2. *Environmental obstacles:* Sometimes a needs analysis will show you that lack of skills is not the problem. Instead, it is poor workflow design, poor systems, poor plant or machine layout that undermines productivity.
3. *Incentives:* Again, you might discover through needs analysis, by interviewing both workers and supervisor, problems that call for systematic changes, not training. For example, employees are not properly rewarded, or sloppy performers are not disciplined.
4. *Motivation:* Incentives are external factors affecting behaviour. Motivation is internal. Therefore, the needs analysis will focus on how employees feel about their jobs, their values, their confidence levels - information that will help you devise training solutions.

Tools for conducting training needs analysis

We can use one or more of the following tools:

- *Existing data:* Examine records of how well standards are being met in many areas, from performance appraisals to quality to number of complaints or defects.
- *Interviews:* Call supervisors on an informal basis and ask them what problems they're having. Speak in person to employees, customers, managers.
- *Focus groups:* Get together a small group of workers, supervisors, engineers, quality control people, and have

them share in a directed discussion of the area understand. Ask probing questions, and then listen carefully while the participants come up, areas of agreement and disagreements, communication failures, conflicts, and feelings.

- *Experts:* Confer with engineers, designers and quality control experts, both within and outside the company, when attempting to pin down the optimal of performance.
- *Best performers:* Find out from your best workers how and why they are doing the job correctly. If they are more highly motivated or have found a ways others can adopt the same methods.
- *Surveys:* Use surveys late in your research to pinpoint the focus you're getting from earlier studies.

Results expected from needs analysis

Needs analysis should have accomplishes the following:

- Identified a specific training deed
- Outlined optimal — the best performance
- Defined actual — the current state of employees' aptitudes
- Discovered employee feelings about training
- Elicited useful information from your best performing employees.

Assessment Techniques/Ways of Discovering Training Needs

There are certain tools employed by organizations and training centers to assess the training needs of the organization. By identifying these areas an organization can assess the total training needs of the unit. The following techniques are used.

1. ***Identify organizational and production problems***

   (a) *Low productivity:* This is an area, which needs greater concentration on the part of the organization. Enough return should come to the organization in the form of total production. Productivity per employee must alone enhance total production. A low productivity of an employee can signal the training needs.

(b) *High cost:* An organization has to keep its cost of production to a lower level to increase its profit and make the product competitive in the market. So high cost of production will warrant the need to give training to the employees.

(c) *Poor material control:* The material manager should see that materials are not wasted, or over stocking is not made and huge investment is not locked on materials. Training in this line to the employees is a perfect way of materials control.

(d) *Excessive scrap and waste:* Raw materials are always scarce and sometimes costly. So the production manager and materials manager must ensure that the use of raw materials will not lead to huge scrape and waste. Training can do good in this respect.

(e) *Excessive labor management strife:* This is an important area to be taken into account in any organization. The labor management relations must be cordial and any strain may lead to closing of the unit and production will be affected. An effective training can guarantee cordial labor management relationship.

(f) *Excessive grievances:* Any employee will have grievances of his own relating to his job and family. His grievances in the factory must be set right by the organization. Training can help both the organization and the employee to solve the grievances.

(g) *Poor discipline:* Employees should work with discipline in their units. So that total production and productivity will increase. Through a system of training discipline of employees can be enhanced.

(h) *High employee turnover:* Employee turnover means changing the job or switching to various jobs by an employee. A training programme can cut the employee turnover.

(i) *High absenteeism:* Absenteeism comes in the form of taking leave by the employee frequently and at times when the presence of the employee is needed. Such absenteeism can be controlled by training, which can explain the results of absenteeism to the employees.

(j) *Delayed production:* Production schedule of an organization must be reached perfectly to face competition, meet the demands of the consumers and to meet the export needs. Delayed production can be tackled by adequate training to the employees.

2. ***Analyze jobs and employees***

(a) *Job analysis:* Job analysis explains the needs of jobs, job requirements and training needs of employees. A training process can make the job analysis more effective and fruitful.

(b) *Career Plans:* Job enrichment, transfer, promotion.

(c) *Employee appraisal:* Through this method we can discover the training needs of an organization. Individual training needs of employees can also discover the training needs.

(d) *Testing:* By making random checks or routine tests, among the employees, the training needs of total employees could be assessed.

3. ***Collect employee and managerial options***

By means of collecting the opinions of the employees and allowing the managerial options towards training, the training needs of an organization can be assessed. Interviews can be conducted on individual employees and the training needs can be discovered.

4. ***Anticipate future problems***

Any organization should forecast the future problems that could arise from corners like consumers, competitors, governments, and multinational companies. The following problems must be anticipated properly, for which needed training could be identified.

(a) *Expansion of business:* Any organization must have expansion programmes in its agenda. While expanding the business, number of factors like future demand for the product, cost, competitor's ability, etc. should be considered. These factors will throw needed training to the employees.

(b) *New product new service:* Whenever new product or services are introduced they will create training areas to the organization.

(c) *New designs:* To satisfy the variety needs of the consumers an organization must concentrate on giving new training to the employees.

(d) *New plants:* Expansion of the organization through new plants will warrant the organization to take factors like capital, personnel, etc. to consideration for which training is needed.

(e) *New technology:* New technology is needed to update the production process and increase total production and productivity. This may throw new areas for training.

Checklist of Problems

The problems that may arise in a company may lead to the training necessity. Such problems are as follows:

1. Customer's complaints
2. Delays caused by errors and mistakes
3. Excessive time taken to finish jobs or orders or supply parts
4. Law output

5. Excessive absenteeism or unpunctuality
6. High labour turnover
7. High accident frequency
8. Excessive maintenance cost
9. Frequent bottlenecks in production
10. Excessive holdups through slow paper work or procedures
11. Errors resulting from instructions not clearly understood
12. People receiving instructions from more than one person
13. Poor communications
14. Ignorance of safety rules
15. Untidiness of workplace
16. Ignorance of company rules
17. Excessive wear and tear on equipment
18. Employees' difficulty in mastering new job or new equipment
19. Lack of flexibility in labor force, no substitutes for absentees
20. Too much waste, scrap
21. Specifications not followed
22. Standards of quality not met
23. Errors caused by careless measuring
24. Employees' lack of interest in the work
25. Failure to realize important or minor details

Data Sources Used in Training Needs Assessment

Organizational Analysis:

- Organizational goals and objectives
- Personnel inventories
- Skills inventories
- Organization climate indexes
- Efficiency indexes
- Changes in systems or subsystems (e.g., equipment)

- Management requests
- Exit interviews
- Management-by-objectives or work
- Planning systems

Job/Task Analysis:

- Job descriptions
- Job specifications
- Performance standards
- Performing the job
- Work sampling
- Reviewing literature on the job
- Asking questions about the job
- Training committees
- Analysis of operating problems

Person Analysis:

- Performance appraisal data
- Work sampling
- Interviews
- Questionnaires
- Tests (KASOCs)
- Altitude surveys
- Training progress
- Assessment centres
- Critical incidents

Pitfalls that should be avoided when designing training systems

The training efforts should always be shaped by the needs analysis and corporate strategies. Following guidelines can be used to avoid the most common training pitfalls.

1. *Don't use training as a screening device:* Training should challenge your employees, but not be a hurdle. The goal is for all trainees to succeed.

2. *Don't try to cover large areas at once:* People learn best when information is presented small bits.
3. *Don't confuse training and education:* The purpose of training is strictly to produce a measurable improvement in productivity. Encourage your employees to continue their education at their own expense and on their own time.
4. *Provide short-term rewards:* There can be monetary or simply the praise and encouragement of managers or trainers.
5. *Set training priorities:* Don't limit training to areas where the solutions are most obvious. Look at problems where the biggest gap between desired and actual performance exists—for the behaviour that is the most common or most costly in terms of lost productivity—and seek solutions there. You cannot setup training systems to address all performance problems. Choose those that will be the most cost-effective. Don't expect immediate results. While short-term training needs sometimes do arise, the training efforts of some companies consist of nothing but quick fixes. Too often, this amounts to aimlessly throwing money at a problem, money that is usually wasted. Thorough needs analysis and systematic training design are the only cost- effective approaches to solving these problems.

Summary

- TNA is a rational way of deciding what kind of training activity to undertake, to make an analysis of the entire organization (people, job technology, etc) and to identify trouble spots where training may help.
- There are organizational, operations, and individual analysis in TNA.
- There are certain tools employed by organizations and training centers to assess the training needs of the organization. By identifying these areas an organization can assess the total training needs of the unit.

Self-Learning Activity

Try to answer the following questions on your own:

1. What are the objectives of TNA?
2. Write about organizational analysis.
3. Describe various tools used in TNA.

9

PLANNING TRAINING PROGRAMMES

Important Considerations

Like any other function of management, planning as a first step is also recognized in training. Before initiating a training programme, proper planning must be made with regard to the needs of the training, budget allocation for training, training establishment, etc. Further, the following considerations must be weighed during planning training programme.

1. *Outlook of the organization towards training*

   The organization must have a positive outlook about training the employees. It should consider training as an investment on the employees and the expenditure on training is going to be productive in achieving the goals of the organization.

2. *Preparedness for training*

   During the planning stage, the organization must prepare itself for training by means of entrusting the training responsibility to a responsible executive. Enough budget allocation must also be made for training. Infrastructure facilities must also be built adequately for training, if training is conducted within the organization.

3. *Organization for training*

To conduct training programmes for employees, organizations have different organizational arrangements. They are as follows:

(a) In small companies, training is to a greater extent done on the basis on the job variety and it is done by the line supervisors. If personnel department exists in such small organizations, training will become the responsibility of the personnel manager.

(b) In big companies, separate training section is established within the personnel or industrial relations department. Here, training and management development functions are combined in one section.

(c) In very many countries, we can find separate training centers or training colleges have been established for various categories of employees. The purpose of such training centers is to train the employees throughout the year. In the cooperative circle, many countries have two or three tier cooperative training institutes or colleges.

In choosing a training center, the following considerations must be made:

(a) *Trainer:* Right type of trainers must be selected for individual training.

(b) *Trainees:* The number of trainees and the individuals who are deputed for training must also be systematically planned.

(c) *Curriculum:* The training center must prepare the curriculum suited to the needs of the trainees and the tastes of the organization.

(d) *Training material:* Needed training materials must be prepared prior to the launching of the training programmes.

(e) *Methods and techniques:* Training methods and training techniques must also be selected prior to the training programme.

(f) *Timing and sequence:* The total training period must be decided in consultation with the organization and the training period must also be broken into daily programme with details.

(g) *Location:* The location of the training programme to be conducted by the training center must be decided (within the training center premise or outside).

(h) *Physical facilities:* Physical facilities relating to accommodation, cafeteria, travel, library, etc must be properly planned.

Elements of Successful Training

Successful training is one, which will give fuller benefits for the money spent on training. The stakeholders of the training programme namely, the organization, the trainee, and the trainer must get required benefits out of the training. For the organizations training should result in improved work efficiency, cost saving, updating technology and skills. For the trainees, it should result in improved morale, enriching new skills and learning new knowledge. For the trainer, it should give different exposures and improvement in their teaching process.

Those who plan training programmes should assess carefully the training that is needed, who is being training, who will be doing the training, and the best method to use. An additional consideration is the culture needed to encourage people to participate and to support them as they adapt to new ways of working. If employees are unable to use new skills and ideas after participating in training programmes, disappointment and frustration result and can lead to poor morale.

Human resource managers are often responsible for meeting an organization's training needs. They may be expected to provide the training or to be a source of information about training needs. To determine who needs training in the organization supervisors can draw information from several sources.

Guidelines for Effective Training Programmes

- Content must be relevant to the learner.
- Content should be realistic.
- Trainee should see the benefits.
- Rewards should be a part of the programme.
- Start small and show, don't overwhelm
- Build confidence with early successes.
- Let the learners participate avidly.
- Practice makes perfect if the practice is correct.
- Provide constructive feedback during practice.
- Protect self-esteem.
- Mistakes are expected.
- Provide the opportunity for feedback about the programme.

Organization or group plans: Strategic plans are the basis for forecasting human resource needs. When those future needs are compared with employee demographics and skill inventories, deficiencies can be remedied through training or retraining of current employees or by hiring new people.

Employee records: Employee application and test records are a source of information about new employees and their training needs. Demographics indicate that basic skill remediation is vital for today's workforce and will remain so in the future.

Performance appraisal and career plan: Employees with potential for advancement or a desire to try another area within the company are prime candidates for training because they are motivated to learn new job skills. Training may also be needed for employees whose performance has been evaluated as below acceptable levels. Sometimes a review of appraisals reveals that an entire work group has similar problems and requires corrective training.

Observation: Individual or group has an increase in the number of accidents, more wasted materials high absenteeism or turnover rates, poor morale, or a productivity, supervisors need to evaluate the situation to decide if training might help. Observation is an important skill for supervisors, and it can be improved with practice. Supervisors must watch for signals that point to a need for training or retraining of employees.

Results of training: The evaluations and outcomes of training programmes may indicate that more training or a different kind of training is required. Participants often make suggestions about additional training needs. The extent to which trainees transfer what they have learned to the workplace situation also tells supervisors whether addition training is needed.

Readiness to learn: Trainees must want to learn what is being taught, or the best-planned programme cannot succeed. They must recognize the benefits of the training and its relevance to their own success. They must also be capable of learning. Supervisors should clarify and share criteria for training programmes so that all of those who are eligible understand them and can assess their own needs.

Functions Relating to Planning of Training

1. *Determination of training needs:* Through training needs assessment, the training needs of the organization as well as the individuals must be decided.
2. *Development of overall plans:* Through this process, the objectives of training programme must be fixed and responsibilities relating to training must be assigned to the relevant staff.
3. *Development of training programme in consultation with line executives:* Line executives of departments like materials, marketing, finance, HRM, etc have greater say in arranging training programmes. They must be consulted during planning period.
4. *Collection of training material, etc.:* The training center must collect enough training material, curriculum, books, and audio-visual aids well before the training programme.

5. *Selection of course and instructors:* The type of training to be given and the details must be planned properly. If training is given within the organization, the instructors must be selected and given orientation.
6. *Training of certain personnel as instructors:* When training is given within the organization, suitable personnel must be selected as trainers and they must be given training.
7. *Administration and coordination of all training programmes:* Training programmes relating to various departments must be coordinated and unity must be maintained in all respects.
8. *Evaluation of training:* No training ends without evaluation. So, evaluation procedure must be decided even during the planning stage.

Training Director

In exclusive training sections under personnel department, the training director takes the responsibility of training. The functions of a training director are as follows:

1. Determination of training needs.
2. Development of overall plans, objectives and assignment of responsibilities.
3. Development of training programmes in consultation with line executives.
4. Collection and preparation of training materials, outlines, curricula, textbooks, and audio-visual aids.
5. Selection of qualified instructors.
6. Training of certain personnel who are designated as instructors.
7. Administration and coordination of all training programmes.
8. Evaluation of effectiveness of the training programmes.

Line Training Responsibilities

Top management executives have the responsibility to authorize basic training policies. They should also review and approve the broad outlines of training plans and programmes. The training budget must also be approved by them. They should also approve the training programmes prepared by the training director. The line managers must also approve the training programme.

With regard to the lower line management, staff like foremen, supervisors, etc must recognize the training problems that exist in their departments. They can also participate in special training programmes for the successful running of on-the-job training activity. They must also select the people to be sent for training.

Summary

- Like any other function of management, planning as a first step is also recognized in training. Before initiating a training programme, proper planning must be made with regard to the needs of the training, budget allocation for training, training establishment, etc.
- There are guidelines for effective training programme, and functions of planning the training.

Self-Learning Activity

Try to answer the following questions on your own:

1. Write short note on Organization for Training.
2. What are the guidelines for an effective training programme?

10

Job Analysis

Definition

According to Michael Jucius, "Job analysis refers to the process of gathering information about the operations, duties, and organizational aspects of jobs in order to write up specifications or job descriptions".

As per "Job analysis is the process of studying and collecting job information relating to operation and responsibilities of a specific job".

Edwin Flippo

Meaning

Job analysis means, the careful determination of what the workers do on a job, as determined by a trained analyst. It is a useful tool for assessing the training needs in an organization. Fifty or twenty or other items of information in addition to the statement of duties are included in the analysis. The exact list of these items varies with the judgment of the person planning the study and with the purpose to which the information is put several items of identifications, such as the name of the plant, industry, department, job titles and alternative titles and number of persons working at the job, are included.

The primary purpose of job analysis is to determine exactly what the worker does. The analysis also ascertains the way the work is done, how it is done and the skill involved. Also included are minimum and desirable qualifications of training and experience, working conditions, physical requirements, number of persons supervised, supervisor and character of supervision received, relationship to the jobs, tools, process used, qualifications found desirable for placement on the job including intelligence and dexterity. Job analysis helps to identify the training needs of employees and organizations.

Categories of Job Analysis

Job analysis may be divided into three categories, namely job content, job context, and worker requirements.

1. ***Job Content***

   It refers to workers' job activities, actually what workers do on the job. While gathering information about the tasks, the job analyst seeks to determine what the worker does, the purpose of the action, and the tools, equipments, or machinery used in the process. He may also gather additional information about tasks, such as their importance, the expected performance level and the type of training needed by a new worker in order to perform the task satisfactorily.

2. ***Job Context***

   It refers to the conditions under which a person's job is performed and the demands such job impose upon the individual. The job context information are reporting relationships, supervision received, judgment about how the job will be carried out, authority the worker has with respect to hiring, firing, disciplining, and budgeting, personal contacts the worker comes in contact, working conditions in the factory, physical demands, and personal demands.

3. ***Work Requirements***

   This refers to the knowledge, skill, ability, personal characteristics, and credentials needed for effective job performance. These terms are further developed as knowledge, skill, and ability.

Job Analysis and the Manager's Job

A manager responsible for conducting job analysis for the positions they supervise use an interview approach to data collection. When interviewing the workers, the following guidelines are suggested.

1. *State the purpose of the interview:* The workers must understand the reasons for the interview.
2. *Structure the interview:* The interview can be structured to focus on job content, job context, and work requirements.
3. *Steer the interview:* Ask the worker to describe the job in his own words and insist on a thorough description on each activity.
4. *Record the interview:* The interview can be recorded by means of note taking. Some type of shorthand can be followed and the notes must be re-written after the interview.
5. *Close the interview:* Summarize the information collected from the worker and close the interview.

Documenting Job Analysis Information

While documenting job analysis information, an approach called VERJAS (Versatile Job Analysis System) is followed. This is a job description contains a list of duties, tasks, task ratings for importance and for needed training, job context descriptions, and a list of competencies needed for the job. When using this approach, the following guidelines should be followed:

1. *Identify duties:* The first step in VERJAS is to identify the duties or functions of the job.
2. *Identify tasks:* This is tasks associated with each duty. A task is defined as "an activity a worker performs to create

a product or a service that they will use in performing another task or that someone else will use". The task statements should describe the action, object of the action, expected output of the action, and tools and equipments used to accomplish the activity.

3. *Evaluate tasks:* Each task statement must be evaluated on four scales, namely performance at entry, training mode, importance level, and reason for important/critical ratings.
4. *Evaluate job context:* This is to analyze the context of the job by completing the appropriate section of the form.
5. *Evaluate worker competencies (Worker requirements)* - The final step of VERJAS is to record the needed worker competencies. There are two types of competencies, namely basic competencies and special competencies (needed for superior job performance).

Scope or Contents of Job Analysis

The scope of job analysis refers to the kinds of information that must be obtained in connection with it. There are certain types of data that are included in most analysis. The job analysis process seeks to provide information in the following major areas:

1. *Job identification:* It includes job title, name, and its code number.
2. *Distinctive characteristic of the job:* It includes job location, physical setting, supervision, union justification, hazards, and discomforts of the job.
3. *What the typical worker does?* It includes—
   (a) Specific operations and tasks that make up the assignment
   (b) Their relative timing and importance
   (c) The simplicity, routine, or complexity of tasks
   (d) Responsibilities for other, for property, for funds
   (e) Products made or services performed

4. *Materials and equipments used:* They include machines, tools, equipments, and work aids used such as metals, plastics, grain, yarns, lathes, electronic tools, etc.
5. *How the job is performed:* It specifies the nature of operations such as handling, feeding, removing, drilling, driving, etc. It also includes error analysis, work standards, and work measurements such as time taken for each task.
6. *Requiring personnel activities*: It includes—
   - (*a*) Personnel features such as personality, interest, physical strength, aptitude, mental capabilities, social skills, etc.
   - (*b*) Education, training, and apprenticeship required
   - (*c*) Work experience
7. *Job relationships*: It includes—
   - (*a*) Opportunities for advancement
   - (*b*) Patterns of promotion to and from
   - (*c*) Directions or leadership from and for other jobs
   - (*d*) Usual sources of employees
8. *Job context:* It includes—
   - (*a*) Work schedule
   - (*b*) Financial and non-financial incentives
   - (*c*) Physical working conditions
   - (*d*) Organizational and social environment
9. *Work related activities:* These include—
   - (*a*) Human behaviour such as physical actions and communication
   - (*b*) Elemental motions for methods analysis
   - (*c*) Personal job demands such as energy expenditure

Uses of Job Analysis

Job information collected from job analysis has many important applications, as follows:

1. *Manpower planning:* Job analysis helps in determining the number and kinds of jobs and the qualifications needed to fill these jobs.
2. *Recruitment, selection, and placement:* To carryout an employment programme, it is necessary to have clear statements of work to be performed by employees who will fill these jobs. Basically, the goal is to match the job requirements with the workers aptitudes and abilities. So for this purpose full job information is necessary.
3. *Equal employment opportunity:* Equal employment opportunity laws, regulations, and court orders have made accurate job analysis of extreme importance. The burden of proof is upon the employer to justify an educational requirement.
4. *Establishing proper rates of pay:* This involves the determination of the relative worth of jobs within the organization by means of the technique called job evaluation and a comparison of wages paid inside the organization compared to the wage paid in other companies. The purpose of job evaluation here is to ensure internal pay equity of one job to other.
5. *Redesign the job:* Jobs may be redesigned to improve the methods, reduce errors and duplication of efforts and to improve the performance of the employee.
6. *Employee training and management development:* New employees are provided with job descriptions, which help them in orienting with the new job. Job information is also helpful to those who administer training and development programmes.
7. *Performance appraisal:* Job analysis data helps to perform the performance appraisal perfectly.
8. *Safety and health:* Job analysis provides an opportunity to identify hazardous conditions and unhealthy environmental factors so that, corrective measures can be taken.

Summary

- Job analysis means, the careful determination of what the workers do on a job, as determined by a trained analyst. It is a useful tool for assessing the training needs in an organization.
- In addition to the statement of duties, the exact list of items varies with the judgment of the person planning the study and with the purpose to which the information is put several items of identifications, such as the name of the plant, industry, department, job titles and alternative titles and number of persons working at the job, are included.

Self-Learning Activity

Try to answer the following questions on your own:

1. Define Job Analysis.
2. How do organizations document the job analysis information?

11

JOB DESCRIPTION

Definition

As per Edwin Flippo: "A job description is an organized, factual statement of the duties and responsibilities of a specific job. In brief, it should tell what is to be done, how is it done and why".

Meaning

It is a systematic summary of facts. It is a written statement of what the jobholder does, how it is done and why it is done. It should accurately portray job content, environment, work performed, the responsibilities involved, the skill or training required conditions under which the job is done, relations with other jobs and personal requirements of the job. It is descriptive in nature. It defines the purpose and scope of a job. It aims to differentiate a job from other job. It gives a clear idea of what the job is.

Like the job analysis, job description also helps in identifying training needs and areas of training in an organization.

VERJAS (Versatile Job Analysis System)

A typical general purpose job description contains the following sections — job identification, job summary, essential functions, and worker requirements. A systematic method of recording job information is called as VERJAS (Versatile Job Analysis System). Some of the commonly used special purpose job descriptions are as follows:

1. ***Ability Requirements Approach (ARA)***

   It is a systematic method of recording job analysis information in which a job analyst specified needed abilities from a list of all the possible abilities needed for any job. ARA is often used for employee selection and to set medical standards for jobs.

2. ***Position Analysis Questionnaire (PAQ)***

   This is a systematic method of recording job analysis information in which the behavioural dimensions of a job are specified. Overall job dimensions on the PAQ are as follows:

   (a) having decisions, communicating and general responsibilities

   (b) operating machines and equipments

   (c) performing clerical and related activities

   (d) performing technical or related activities

   (e) performing service or related activities

   (f) working regular day versus other work schedules

   (g) performing routine or respective activities

   (h) being aware of work environment

   (i) engaging physical activities

   (j) supervising/directing/estimating

   (k) public, customer or related contacts

   (l) working in an unpleasant/hazardous environment

   (m) miscellaneous

3. ***Critical Incident Technique (CIT)***

   CIT was developed in the military during the Second World War as a means of identifying critical factors in human performance in a variety of military situations. The rationale for this technique, according to its originator, John Flanagan is as follows. "The principal objective of job analysis procedures should be the determination of critical requirements. These requirements include those that have been demonstrated to make the difference between success and failure in carrying out an important part of the job assigned in a significant number of instances. Too often, statements regarding job requirements are merely lists of all the desirable traits of human beings. These are practically no help in selecting, classifying or training individuals for specific jobs".

CIT is a specific work behaviour that may determine success or failure in executing a job. The CIT requires the job analyst to collect critical incidents from people familiar with the job. The incidents are usually collected in the form of stories or anecdotes that depict successful and unsuccessful job behaviours. The stories are then condensed to a single statement, which "captures the essence" of the story.

Contents of Job Description

1. *Job title and location:* These designate the job and the organizational unit in which it is located. Some standardization of job titling is desirable.
2. *Job summary:* This is included in most job descriptions to give the reader a quick capsule explanation of the job. It is usually one or two sentences in length.
3. *Job duties:* A comprehensive listing of duties is included together with an indication of the frequency of occurrence or percentage of time devoted to each major duty. Always includes what the jobholder does along with some indication of how he performs the tasks.
4. *Machines, tools and equipment:* A listing of all the tooling and work aids used in the job.
5. *Materials, products, services:* Raw materials used and produced made or services performed.

6. *Supervision given:* For supervisory and group leader jobs, the number of persons supervised and their job titles are given.
7. *Relation to other jobs:* Identify jobs from which persons can be promoted into this job. Also state the jobs to which persons in this job can be promoted.
8. *Mental skills:* Includes various mental skills such as ability to interpret complex data and ideas, resourcefulness, and ability to influence others.
9. *Physical demand:* Kind and amount of physical exertion. Normal working position such as sitting or standing.
10. *Physical skills:* Examples are manual dexterity and eye-hand-foot coordination.
11. *Responsibilities:* Examples are responsibility for product and equipment and responsibility for preventing monetary loss to organization.
12. *Working conditions:* Environmental conditions such as cold, heat, dust, noise.
13. *Hazards:* Typical work hazards encountered (e.g. broken bones) and probability of occurrence.
14. *Education:* Identify specific kinds of reasoning, language, and mathematical skills required and amount of schooling needed to provide such skills.
15. *Vocational Preparation:* This includes vocational education, apprenticeship training, prior work experience, and in-plant job training.

Summary

- Job description is a systematic summary of facts. It should accurately portray job content, environment, work performed, the responsibilities involved, the skill or training required conditions under which the job is done, relations with other jobs and personal requirements of the job. It is descriptive in nature.

- It defines the purpose and scope of a job. It aims to differentiate a job from other job. It gives a clear idea of what the job is.
- Like the job analysis, job description also helps in identifying training needs and areas of training in an organization.

Self-Learning Activity

Try to answer the following questions on your own:

1. Write short note on Critical Incident Technique.
2. What are the contents of Job Description?

12

DESIGNING TRAINING PROGRAMME

Designing training programme denotes the strategy and planning through which training programme could be conducted effectively. In order to deliver real business benefits, training must be designed to be relevant to the organization's objectives and needs. Whenever employees' performance falls short, steps must be taken to improve the performance. Where required levels of skill and ability are not present, improvement is also needed and training design for groups or individuals will be necessary to rectify the performance or skill deficit. The effectiveness of training will be ultimately evaluated in terms of the organization's success in achieving its goals and objectives.

Preliminary steps

While designing the training programme the following preliminary steps are needed.

1. Enlist the support of all the concerned
2. Examine the job
3. Describe the job in simple terms
4. Analyze the job-training requirements by:
   (a) Identifying skills and knowledge
   (b) Breaking down skills and knowledge in detail required

(c) Summarizing job training requirement in a syllabus.

Training Policy and Strategy

All training should be designed as part of training policy and strategy. Training policy forms the backdrop of all decisions about training. Training strategy is an essential reference for the annual training plan. Training policy and strategy must meet the expectations of the organization. The training function need to help the organization develop a strong training culture, which positions training and development as an important resource to the organizations. Efforts will be needed to:

1. raise awareness of training and development and their benefits.
2. create interest in training as a way of addressing and meeting business problems and needs such as competitiveness.
3. convince the employees that training and development are valuable to them and to the organization.
4. encourage the individuals to value the learning opportunities presented by training.
5. develop a culture of continuous learning and development.

Planning Training

Training should only be carried out when there is an identified performance need. This need can be identified in a number of ways such as training needs analysis, request for help by managers, planned change, etc. Training outcomes should be specified at the outset and planned in terms of:

1. specific aims and plans with which the training is to be linked (development plans).
2. the training purpose, i.e., what will be different or better in performance if the training is successful (development objectives).

3. the learning to be achieved, i.e. what individual should know or be able to do as a result of undergoing the training (learning objectives)
4. how effective and results will be measured (evaluation objectives).

Who are to be involved in designing the training?

The role of training function is to design or have designed and put into place, training, which meets the performance needs of the organization. Its role is also to use its expertise to help all stakeholders contribute effectively to the training design. The stakeholders and their expectations are indicated below.

Sl. No.	Stakeholders	Stakeholder expectations
1.	Senior management	• Improved competitiveness • Improvement in specific performance • An approach to coincide organizations' strategy • Careful use of resources — finance and human • Training, which will reflect best practice • Proposals for cost-effective evaluation
2.	Line managers (as recipients of training)	• Training appropriate to their needs • Assurance that training is designed for them • Clearly defined business and learning objectives • Minimum disruption • Clear benefits for them and for the organization • Improved skills, abilities and knowledge

(Contd…)

3.	Line managers (as managers of staff receiving training from others)	• To be consulted • Involvement at an early design stage • Minimum disruption to their work • Clearly defined objectives and benefits • Choice of method, which suits their staff • Training, which will reflect best practice • Demonstrable contribution to effectiveness
4.	Line managers who have to offer the training themselves	• To be equipped to deliver the training solution • Complete support in terms of material, training design, evaluation criteria and methods • To be protected from failure • Appropriate delivery methods • Clarity about monitoring and reporting
5.	Personnel function	• To be consulted/involved • Training designed will meet – Identified organizational needs – Any legislative requirements, for example health and safety – Any budgetary constraints • To be informed at appropriate stages
6.	Workforce in general	• Assurance that trainers understand their work • Training, which is relevant to them and their needs • Clear explanation and positioning of training offered • Some personal benefits, for example knowledge, skill, etc • Honest feedback
7.	Customers – internal or external	• A competent workforce • A workforce, which understands customers' needs • Working methods, which enhance customer service

Contents of Training Programme

The following contents are to be carefully considered in designing training programme.

1. ***Statement of Objectives***

The objectives of the programme must be clearly set down. This will help to ensure that only those items are included, which help the trainee to achieve the learning or the standard required. The statement should include the following:

(a) For whom the programme is written (training specifications).

(b) What the trainee is expected to be able to do at significant stages.

(c) Standard of performance to be achieved.

(d) How this standard will be tested.

(e) The situation in which these standards will be tested.

3. ***Practical considerations affecting the design of the training programmes***

While designing the training programmes, it must be designed to meet the objectives of the organization and all the concerned. This approach has the following advantages—a standard is set; the programme designer is dealing with one thing at a time and future adjustments are made more easily. The most common practical considerations, which may affect the training programmes, are cost, urgency, availability of space, availability of instructors, and availability of materials. The availability of materials includes manuals and other written materials, case studies, films and film strips, visual aids, machinery and other manual aids.

3. ***The place where the training is to be carried out***

Depending on the type of job for which the training is being prepared, there will be elements of the training, which are done off-the-job and which are best done on-the-job. The mixture will depend on the nature of the job, in-company facilities, and the availability of external courses.

(a) *In-company, On-the-Job:* The proportion of the programme devoted to this type of training is largely determined by the type of the job to be learned. On-the-Job training may be applicable to more complex jobs, which can be broken down into simple steps. This training can be fully effective only when — the person giving the instruction is fully trained, those parts of the job best suited to Off-the-Job training are not dealt with On-the-Job, and there is full induction of the trainee into the work situation.

(b) *In-company, supernumerary:* This training is suitable when Off-the-Job training is to be followed by a period during which the trainee will develop skill at the place of work. Supernumerary training is also suitable when the trainee needs broad experience of several types of work.

(c) *In-company, Off-the-Job:* Off-the-job training is used

  (i) to establish the self-confidence of the trainee.

  (ii) when the tasks, which the trainee will face do not occur in any coherent order.

  (iii) when some of these tasks, the trainee will be required to perform occur only infrequently at the place of work.

  (iv) when the slow speed at which the employee can perform the job would disrupt production.

  (v) when the trainee needs a lot of knowledge to do the job.

(d) *External Courses:* The training facilities of external bodies are used when:

  (i) The skills and knowledge learned internally need to be supplemented by external courses.

  (ii) The company has not comparable facilities internally.

  (iii) The company does not have suitable trainers.

  (iv) There are too few trainees for the training.

  (v) There is an advantage in mixing with the employees of other companies.

4. ***Timing the programme***

Timing may be realistic and flexible. Realistic because:

(a) the trainee needs sufficient time to learn.

(b) the time costs money.

Flexible because:

(a) trainees vary in the speed at which they learn.

(b) trainers vary in the speed at which they promote the learning.

(c) conditions under which learning takes place vary from day to day.

5. ***Pace of the programme***

The level of ability of the trainees determine the general pace at which skill and knowledge can be fed to them but there are other considerations like, the length of the time elapsed since the trainees were last in a training situation, the stages at which the rate of learning slows down, and the speed at which the trainee will be expected to perform his job at the place of work.

6. ***Level of instruction***

The level of instruction must match the trainees' abilities. Sometimes, the material to be learned is at high level and sometimes it will be at low level. The question of level needs to be assessed carefully.

7. ***Need for feedback***

At frequent intervals during the training, both the trainer and the trainees must know how they are progressing. The trainer needs to know whether:

(a) the items to be learned are being learned.

(b) there are gaps in his instruction.

(c) there are gaps in the programme.

(d) there are slower trainees who need attention.

(e) there are quicker trainees who need extra work.

The trainee needs to know whether:

(a) he has correctly understood the information given (knowledge).

(b) he can use the information on a job of work (skill).

With regard to feedback, whatever the form of test, it must be carefully devised with the following points in mind.

(a) The objective of the part of the programme being tested.

(b) The standard expected of the trainee.

(c) The type of training.

(d) The place at which the test is to be set.

(e) The ease with which the test can be marked or judged.

8. ***Choice of the training technique***

The choice of the training technique should be made with the following:

(a) The end result to be achieved.

(b) The person who is to give the particular session.

(c) The type of training.

(d) The time of day.

(e) The technique used for other programme.

Delivery Considerations

Training design can be successfully undertaken after the following factors are considered.

1. ***Training need***

   (a) Is this concerned with knowledge acquisition, skill development or attitude change?

   (b) Is it about personal development or team development?

   (c) Does it require group learning or individual learning?

   (d) What is the subject matter and how much expertise does this need?

   (e) What methods are suitable for this particular topic?

   (f) What experience is available in the design of training?

(g) Will the most suitable training approach work well in the circumstance?

2. ***Target audience***
   (a) How much do they already know?
   (b) How receptive are they likely to be to the training?
   (c) What level should the training be set?
   (d) What are the groups' learning preferences?
   (e) What demands on the audience may affect them?
   (f) Are there any special needs?
   (g) What will add credibility to the proposed training?

3. ***Resources available***
   (a) How much time and money can be committed to the training?
   (b) Will expert inputs be required from others?
   (c) What facilities and materials are available?
   (d) How much time is available for the development?
   (e) How is the training to be evaluated?

Choosing Appropriate Training Methods and Media

There are three dimensions in the choice of appropriate training methods and strategies:

1. Range of delivery mechanisms/strategies available
2. Different styles and types of training/learning activity
3. Different training media available

Sl. No.	Mechanisms/Strategy	Possible Approaches
1.	Group training/ group learning	• Lecture • Workshops/seminars • Peer study groups • Action learning sets • Focus groups • Discussion groups • Guided practical activities • Project planning and management

(Contd...)

2.	Coached development on-the-job	• Programme or coaching interventions by manager • 'Sitting next to Nelly' • Support from a sponsor or mentor • Supervised practice • Properly briefed delegation • One-to-one instruction • Work place practices and experimentation • Tasks and projects • Use of personal development plans with feedback from the manager
3.	Self-study	• Distance learning courses • Self-study material, e.g., CD-ROMs • Planned reading/research • Individual written activities and exercises • Video watching • Intranet or internet training • Practical experience linked to learning logs

Pre-Training Preparation

Part of the training design should be to consider the need for pre-training preparation. This will involve reading or pre-course work to ensure that everyone who attempts a course has achieved at least a minimum of understanding of the topic before they get there. Pre-training knowledge tests and checks are also valuable from the evaluation point also. To prove that the training has made a difference, the trainer needs to know where learners are starting from. In terms of training design the trainer needs to be alert to the demands made by:

- Learning
- Behaviour
- Results required

A range of possible training approaches are given below:

Planning in Evaluation

As resources are limited and all training design and activity needs to be justified in terms of what it adds to the organization. Training designers have to be aware of the need to:

(a) justify the investment in training.

(b) ensure that training really has made a difference to the organization and to the individual.

(c) be able to identify area in which further training may be required.

(d) evaluate the training investment in terms of costs vs. bottom-line benefits.

Evaluation aims to make a direct link between the resources allocated to the training and the practical business results, which these achieve. Evaluation should begin during the training design stage and this involves:

(a) deciding which level of evaluation is to be attempted.

(b) deciding what aspects of training need to be evaluated.

(c) choosing the evaluation methods to be used.

(d) identifying what trainers will evaluate and what other in the organization will evaluate.

(e) Costing the evaluation effort as part of the overall training expenditure.

Summary

- Designing training programme denotes the strategy and planning through which training programme could be conducted effectively. In order to deliver real business benefits, training must be designed to be relevant to the organization's objectives and needs.
- There are different considerations in designing training programme: training policy and strategy, contents of training programme, and training approaches.

Self-Learning Activity

Try to answer the following questions on your own:

1. Write about training policy and strategy.
2. What are the possible training approaches?

13

CRITICAL INCIDENT TECHNIQUE AND TECHNOLOGY OF TRAINING PROGRAMMES

Context of CIT

Critical Incident Technique (CIT) is closely related to the personnel function, job-analysis. Job analysis is the process of determining by observation and study and reporting proper information about a specific job. It includes the identification of the tasks performed, the machines and equipment utilized, the materials, products or services involved and training skills, knowledge and personnel traits required of the worker. The work is sub-divided into elements and times are determined for each one. The goal is usually to establish a standard time for each type of work performed by each worker. Work simplification and methods improvement are generally part and parcel of every analysis.

Job analysis employs various tools as follows:

1. Work and time and motion study method;
2. Direct observation;
3. Conducting interviews;
4. Questionnaires on job analysis; and
5. Critical Incident Technique

CRITICAL INCIDENT TECHNIQUE (CIT)

CIT was developed in the military during the Second World War as a means of identifying critical factors in human performance in a variety of military situations. The rationale for this technique, according to its originator, John Flanagan is as follows. "The principal objective of job analysis procedures should be the determination of critical requirements. These requirements include those that have been demonstrated to make the difference between success and failure in carrying out an important part of the job assigned in a significant number of instances. Too often, statements regarding job requirements are merely lists of all the desirable traits of human beings. These are practically no help in selecting, classifying or training individuals for specific jobs".

CIT is a specific work behaviour that may determine success or failure in executing a job. The CIT requires the job analyst to collect critical incidents from people familiar with the job. The incidents are usually collected in the form of stories or anecdotes that depict successful and unsuccessful job behaviours. The stories are then condensed to a single statement, which "captures the essence" of the story.

Definition of CIT

"CIT is a critical approach, which involves gathering data on observed or narrated incidents, which reveal important or critical elements of performance".

Meaning of CIT

It is a device used to find out the right type of training technique. This will coincide with another management technique, Programme Evaluation and Review Technique (PERT). In other words, through CIT technique, we can find the critical path of training. The training technology or the methodology of training has greater bearing in deciding the critical incident path of training. The role of both the sponsoring organization as well as the training centers is important in deciding the right type of training. Various training techniques will be given a free play. Based on the performance of each method, the best one will be selected.

Contents of CIT

1. *Introducing various training techniques:* Under this technique, various training techniques are used by the same instructor or by different instructors. The type of training will be chosen by the organization and the training center.
2. *Give time for each technique to prove its worth:* Every teaching technique will be given adequate time to prove the merit of such training. Training time and its usefulness will also be measured by its utility.
3. *Range of events is wider and the best one is selected:* Each technique of training will be given adequate time to prove its merit or demerits. After giving a long rope, the best one will be selected.
4. *Incident is observed and components are recorded:* Under CIT, each training programme is broken into various components, and each component is observed and recorded.
5. *Conclusions are reached from each component and from each incident:* The sum total of the training programme is taken for selecting the best one. Here, the sequences, objects, tools, and skills are identified and rated.
6. Training incidents are defined objectively and performances are measured without any bias.
7. Recorded incidence form as case studies, which are used again among the trainees for discussion. Such case studies are kept as future reference.

How to Use the Method

1. The trainees who undergo training are used as the important objects of these techniques. They will be asked to note the important techniques of training and asked to note the critical incidence. Explanations for each critical incidence must be given clearly, which are acceptable to the trainers.

2. The trainees will be asked to identify the type of incident they are going to observe. They must draw conclusions on each type of incident.
3. The data collection from the trainees must include the following:
   - *(a)* Describe the incident;
   - *(b)* Give the background of each incident; and
   - *(c)* When the incident occurs, the sequence can be compared with other incidents.

Limitations of CIT

1. *Memory:* The trainees who undergo various types of training must have strong memory. But sometimes, people forget things and some incidents are forgotten. This makes the situations very difficult to compare.
2. *Patience:* One must have patience and must have commitment to various techniques of training. Any shortfall in the patience will make the observations useless.
3. *Recording the incidents:* All the incidents that occur in a training programme must be recorded then and there. But sometimes, people fail to record incidents. But today, using various instruments like tape recorder, video camera, etc, recording can be done accurately.
4. *Objectivity:* All the information collected from the trainees must be analyzed objectively. Any personal biases may make the programme ineffective.
5. *Subjective judgment:* Subjective judgment may occur while categorizing and classifying the elements of incidents. An impartial approach must be given to remove the subjective judgment.

Technology of Training Programmes

Technology of training programme denotes the innovations and new findings that have been introduced in training programmes. The following are the important technology/innovation introduced in training programmes.

1. ***Grid seminars***

Such seminars have two parts. The first part involves each participant is advanced preparation before the session begins. The second part consists of team study sessions in which each participant will be working with several others and explore grid concepts. The pre-work should be done thoroughly to get the best from the seminar. Grid seminars were developed by Dr. Robert Blake and Jane Mouton. The objectives of the seminar are as follows:

(a) Understand the grid style of supervision.

(b) Experience productive teamwork.

(c) Develop skills of solving problems with subordinates.

(d) Clarify personal values and convictions about effective supervision.

(e) Gain deeper insights into personal supervisory style.

(f) Perfect your skills in using the grid approach for solving problems of supervision.

(g) Increase personal motivation to do the best possible job of being effective.

Team learning: Under the grid seminars, the learning activities are centered in the team. This method of study allows people from organizations with similar problems to utilize seminar activities as a means for finding solutions to problems. The training programmes generally employ expert lectures or coaching techniques. The best part of grid seminar is that participants mutually learn from each other rather than from a trainer.

2. ***Supervisory Skills Level (SSL) Technology***

This is a computerized process for the assessment of productivity and work profiles of organizations. It pinpoints areas of excellence as well as areas which need improvement. The SSL technology has been developed by Jorge Chapiro, a management consultant of Argentina and Brazil. The idea behind SSL is that companies can obtain good understanding of the training needs of their supervisors by comparing their performance with other supervisors in other companies. The supervisors are administered statements in a questionnaire stating to agree or disagree with each statement. The final judgments of the questions will reveal the attitude of each supervisor towards his role. The parameters which have significance of the supervisory skills are productivity and climate.

The productivity measures the skills necessary to enable subordinates to achieve the best results possible within the limits of available resources. A high score reflects competence in the supervisory skills like training subordinates, control, safety, discipline, planning and programming.

The climate, another parameter, is an index of the ability to inspire cooperative attitudes. A high score basically, reflects adequate handling of the supervisory skills like work environment, motivation, communication, human relations, and union relations.

3. ***Modular programmes***

A modular programme is one where training materials for supervisory development have been prepared by organizations like ILO. This programme is rich source of training material covering supervisory functions and skills. Some of the features of this training programme are as follows:

(*a*) It is flexible. The self contained modules make it easy for a trainer to mix his own simplified training to suit the needs of his organization.

(*b*) The programme is suitable for training in any type of organization.

(*c*) Since the success of any training programme depends on the trainer, one-third of entire programme is devoted to the trainer.

There are five volumes in the total programme, in all 34 modules containing number of learning elements.

Modular programme for supervisory development	
	I. *Introduction*
Volume I (1-6)	1. Organization and the supervisor
	2. Principles of supervision
	II. *Supervisory techniques*
	3. Planning
	4. Directing and coordinating
	5. Controlling
	6. Work study
Volume II (7-13)	7. Quality control
	8. Finance and cost control
	9. Problem analysis and decision-making
	10. Introducing changes
	11. Communication and records
	12. Individual and group discussion
	13. Management of time
	III. *Main supervisory areas*
Volume III (14-21)	14. Utilization of equipment and facilities
	15. Maintenance management
	16. Materials management
	17. Energy, utilization and auxiliary services
	18. Office supervision
	19. Purchasing
	20. Marketing
	21. Safety and health
	IV. *Supervising people*
Volume IV (22-27)	22. Leadership
	23. Informal groups
	24. Staffing
	25. Motivation
	26. Job evaluation
	27. Performance appraisal

Volume V (28-34)	28. Salary and wage administration 29. Training and development 30. Behaviour in supervision 31. Industrial relations 32. Discipline and morale 33. Complaints and grievances 34. Supervising special groups

4. ***Walkabout***

   Walkabout is an innovative training technology introduced by Asian Institute of Management, Manila, Philippines. According to this technique, a trainee is given training for a particular period and he will be asked to face the challenges in companies. The managerial walkabout must present the trainee with four basic challenges, namely adventure, creativity, practical skills, and logical inquiry.

Summary

- Critical Incident Technique (CIT) is closely related to the personnel function, job-analysis. Job analysis is the process of determining by observation and study and reporting proper information about a specific job. It includes the identification of the tasks performed, the machines and equipment utilized, the materials, products or services involved and training skills, knowledge and personnel traits required of the worker.

Self-Learning Activity

Try to answer the following questions on your own:

1. What are the contents of CIT?
2. Write note on SSL Technology.

14

TRAINING PROCEDURES—STEPS IN TRAINING

Steps in Training

An effective training programme consists of the following steps:

1. *Discover the training needs:* Training needs can be identified by assessing the current and future business conditions and by matching with the skills and resources available and by evaluation of the performance of the people with specific emphasis on areas of improvement.
2. *Establish objectives of the training programmes:* A full assessment must be made of the potential achievement following the training programme and directly attributable to these programmes.
3. *Design*: It is a training system that learners and trainers can implement to meet the learning goals; typically includes identifying learning objectives (which culminate in reaching the learning goals), needed facilities, necessary funding, course content, lessons and sequence of lessons.
4. Develop a training "package" of resources and materials, including, e.g., developing audio-visual, graphics, manuals, etc.

5. Implement the training package, including delivering the training, support group feedback, clarifying training materials, administering tests and conducting the final evaluation. This phase can include administrative activities, such as copying, scheduling facilities, taking attendance data, billing learners, etc.
6. *Getting ready for the job:* This step would specify the type of workers who need to be trained. Are they newcomers or older employees or supervision staff? As much as possible, the training programme should be customer designed to fit individual needs.
7. *Presentation of operations:* This step is the selection of qualified trainees and the identification of training methods. The trainer should build a rapport with the learner and clearly guide him into learning and digesting new knowledge and techniques. Instructions should be given completely, clearly and patiently and a free flow of communication and participation should be encouraged.
8. *Evaluating the effectiveness of the training programme and follow-up:* The effectiveness of the programme can be appraised be written and oral test, by observing the trainees when put to job independently and comparing the results after the training programme was initiated. This should continue until the performance of the worker is up to the expectation of the trainer and then the trainee can be put on his own with reduced supervision.

Factors that Decide the Choice of Training Methods

The next important thing in the training procedure is to decide the choice of training methods.

The following four factors decide the choice of training methods.

1. ***Human Factors***

   (a) *Trainer:* A trainer is the basic source for a successful training. He must have enough knowledge about the field of his training. He must have adequate experience and exposure to deal with the trainees.

(*b*) *Trainees:* The successful method of trainee depends on the type of trainees and their level of knowledge about a particular method of training. Trainees must be given training starting from a low profile to a technical level.

(*c*) *Environment:* Environment relates to the training atmosphere, the place of training physical facilities provided to the trainees.

2. ***Objectives of Training***

(*a*) *Knowledge:* One of the objectives of training can be to inculcate new knowledge. New knowledge should add to the existing knowledge possessed by a trainee.

(*b*) *Skill:* A training method must decide the type of skill to be taught to the trainees. Such skill should be new, productive and goal-oriented.

(*c*) *Attitude:* As noted earlier an effective training must create favorable attitude in an employee towards the organization and working atmosphere.

3. ***Subject Area***

The choice of a trainee must also be decided by the subject area noted below.

(*a*) *Specific subject:* The decision on training is relating to the particular subject to be taught to the trainees. Such subjects can be in the fields of sales promotion, advertisement, promotional aspects, etc.

(*b*) *Interdisciplinary subjects:* The method of training is also decided by the inculcation of interdisciplinary aspects of a problem. During such period of training more than one expert will deal with such subjects.

4. ***Time and Material Factors***

Such factors also decide the method of training to be given to trainees. They are as follows:

(*a*) *Time:* This is the most important factor, which decides the method of training. Training programmes can be arranged from short durations to long durations.

(b) *Finance:* This is another important factor, which decides the choice of training method. In majority of the training programmes the cost is born by the organizations, as such the finance decides the type of training method.

(c) *Teaching facilities:* We cannot expect a training institute to have all types of training facilities. But the method of training depends on the actual facilities available with the training institute.

(d) *Number of persons to be trained:* The size of trainee batch is also a factor that decides the choice of a training method. Because depending on the number of trainees, facilities and other arrangements need to be managed.

(e) *Place of training:* A training programme can be arranged within the campus of the organization or outside places. When training is arranged at outside places travel cost, accommodation, etc. counts a lot. When training is arranged in far away places and hill resorts the cost will be higher.

Time to Train

People need training at many different times in their organizational lives and for a variety of reasons. As the organization evolves and responds to changing economic conditions, it shifts the responsibilities of its employees. Significant and costly problems may result if a firm is not diligent in its efforts to ensure that employees are knowledgeable, capable, and committed to doing their jobs and that they have currently needed skills. A switch to new equipment or procedures is one situation when training is required orientation. Orienting employees means providing them with general information on the company mission, products, and services, policies and regulations, pay and employee benefits and the location and function of other departments. Orienting the employee to job, the workplace, and the people in the work group is the supervisor's responsibility. New workers will need information on departmental procedure, job responsibilities, break times, equipment to be used, and the details of daily and weekly activities.

New technology, new procedures: Training to use new equipment is essential for safety and productivity. Changed procedures to comply with government safety regulation or with court decisions on civil rights often require that employee be trained to understand what is expected of them.

Remediation: Remedial training provides instruction for those who have forgotten the basics of their jobs or never really learnt them. Many workers today also require remediation in such basics as reading, writing, and mathematics.

Apprenticeships: Crafts and trades require training for machinists, printers, carpenters, plumbers, electricians, auto mechanics, and other skilled craft and trade jobs. This usually involves assignment to master craftsman as a teacher for several months or even years. On completing each stage of training, apprentices gain certification for the skill level reached.

Technologically displaced employees: Displaced employees have become an increasingly important concern as more workers lose their jobs to machines and electronic devices. The new jobs available to workers displaced by technology are often more challenging, but they require upgrading of skills or training in a new field.

Development and advancement: Workers today want to learn grow, and advance in their jobs. Boredom, increased absenteeism, and turnover are likely products if this need is not met. It is not enough to offer training, however. Workers also need the opportunity to use the skills that they acquire through training, coaching and development.

Determining the Training Location

One of the elements for successful training is the location. When we talk about training programmes, organizations have their own training centers within the campus or they have established their own training centers in various centers away from the place of the organization. Another process is sending the employees for training to various professional training centers, which are run by government or private organizations. Such training centers give number of training programmes on a routine basis and they collect training fees from the organizations which are sponsoring the trainees. In any case the location of the training center is crucial to make the training programmes successful. The center can be located far away from busy cities, preferably in isolated hill stations or calm places. The following factors are to be considered while choosing the location for a training center:

Number of participants

The number of participants generally determines the training location. A decision about the location should be the trainer's first priority. A crowded venue will not set the proper learning atmosphere. Similarly, a large room for just a few people can also create a barrier to learning.

Size of the training room

The size of the training room will generally depend on two factors; what the room is being used for, and the number of people it has to accommodate. If the room is being used in a classroom setting (a chair with arm table), about 2 to 2.5 square meters per person can be allowed. If the room is being used in a conference setting (chair and full tables), about 2.5 to 3.5 square meters per person can be allowed.

A simple method of estimating the size of the room needed is to multiply the numbers of participants by the area required per person, and then adds a bit for the trainer and his equipments. It is possible to find many other specifications for training room sizes, but they very greatly. An alternative is to use a room that is a size the trainer and group feel comfortable with.

Suitable chair and tables

Suitable chair and tables are needed for a classroom situation. The chair must be comfortable but firm. The table should be narrow and long, about 0.5 by 1.8 meters. This allows two participants per table, both sitting on the same side. Don't tempt to increase the number of participants by sitting them on both sides of the table, as it gets too crowded.

Lighting

The lighting in the room must be arranged to provide for both the trainer's and trainees' requirements. The trainer needs light for the whiteboard to be seen, the trainees also need enough light to be able to take notes if they require. It is upto the individual trainer to determine the lighting requirements.

Background noise

Noise in the background during training can be very destructive to the learning atmosphere. What we can do, is to choose a training location far enough away from the work area to exclude work noises such as machines and telephones.

Access

Access is something that most trainers now take for granted, but we do need to consider how the participants will get to the venue. Will public transport be sufficient? If they use their own transport, will they have some place to park?

Facilities

The facilities that we usually now take for granted must be checked by the trainer. Are tea and coffee making facilities available for morning and afternoon breaks. Do we know access to telephones? Do we know where all the toilets are located? Are all of this information must be passed onto the participants at the beginning of the course. It may also be necessary to find out if there is residential accommodation available.

Air Conditioning

Temperature between 20°C and 25°C is ideal, so air conditioning (or heating) may be a requirement when selecting your training room.

Another thing to remember is that some training aids generate heat during their use, soothe cooling equipment must be able to handle this problem.

Availability of training aids

Training aids must be checked to see that the ones we want to use are available. Some training and conference facilities have only a limited type and quantity. When we establish that the training aids we require are available, check to make sure they are in top working condition.

Spare parts we may need must be located, and one should need to know how to fit them. Overhead projectors, film projectors and slide projectors, for example, might have a globe burn out while we are using them. Prompt replacement means the least disruption.

Public-address system

A public-address system may be advisable in a large conference or seminar situation. It could be a portable type or a built-in system.

Storage areas

Storage areas could be needed for excess equipment, student handouts, training aids not in use, spare parts, training models and many other items.

Training Methods/Procedures

A brief description of training methods/procedures is given below. Please see Chapter 15 for details.

1. *Apprenticeship:* This is a method through which a trainee is given initial training for a period usually 6-12 months. During this period the trainee is given all sorts of knowledge relating to a job.

2. *Career Counseling:* Here the trainees are given an opportunity to work with experienced employees who will identify the areas for improvement and/or advancement.
3. *Coaching:* Coaching is popular means of development and includes working with a trainer. The trainee is given close attention and he learns various methods of skills and the trainee is given continuous feedback and support.
4. *Courses:* Universities and colleges may run specific courses relating to the problems of an organization. Here the trainees are given more amount of theoretical knowledge.
5. *Distance learning:* Distance learning is a method of training where there is no contact between the trainer and trainee. A trainee has to learn through lessons, tapes, etc. This cannot be considered to be an effective method of training.
6. *Internships:* Such method is followed by organizations for newcomers who want to gain experience during vacations. This offers real life experience to a trainee.
7. *Job assignments:* An employee will be assigned a particular job, which can be new to him. Such trainee has to write short reports based on his observations on the new assignment.
8. *Job rotations:* An employee will be assigned a new job completely new to him. Likewise, every frequent period an employee can be assigned new jobs so that one can learn entire aspects of his career.
9. *Lectures:* This is the popular method of training, where a trainer would be giving lecture classes to the trainees. Question-answer methods can also be used here.
10. *Online training:* Using computers, a trainee will be given training on various aspects through websites and other sophisticated techniques.
11. *On-the-job training:* This helps a trainee to get knowledge about the organization's products and services and how they are developed and carried out.

12. *Orientation to new jobs/roles:* This method is similar to that of the apprenticeship method. But here the duration is very short, it may take one or two weeks.
13. *Peer-based methods:* This is based on the exchanging of information, feedback, questions, etc got from the co-workers. Such co-workers who may be friends can teach many things, which other friends may not know.
14. *Self-directed learning:* Here an employee is getting training without anyone's help. He himself takes all efforts to get training.
15. *TV:* This is one of the modern methods of learning. Specific TV programmes are arranged with prior notice on various problems relating to organizations.
16. *Workshops:* This is a method of training, which is organized on the pattern of seminars. Such workshops are conducted for few days and many experts participate in it.
17. *Role play:* This is a method through which a trainee is expected to play the role of others and experience the strain or pleasure of a new job.

Summary

- There are different steps involved in training programme. Human, objectives, subject area, time and materials are some of the factors that decide training methods.
- Organizations determine the location of training by considering certain points as criteria.

Self-Learning Activity

Try to answer the following questions on your own:

1. What are the steps in training programme?
2. Explain the factors that decide the choice of training methods.
3. How do organizations determine the location for training?

15

METHODS OF TRAINING

1. THE LECTURE METHOD

Lecture method is a conventional method of teaching and training and the oldest method of training. Still in many areas of training the lecture method is popularly used and supplemented by other methods of training. There are certain stages needed in preparing and conducting the lecture programme. Such stages are: planning the lecture, preparing the lecture, and delivering the lecture.

Planning the Lecture

Before planning the lecture, four important points must be considered, viz., the audience, the purpose of the talk, the time available, and the subject matter.

(a) *Audience*

Knowledge and characteristics of the audience must be weighed properly. Their background, likes and dislikes, cultural features, level and nature of education must also be taken into consideration. It may be helpful to start with a general discussion or ask questions to get opinions. This approach will give an idea about the knowledge of the group and allow the trainer to make some last minute adjustments, if necessary.

(b) *Purpose of the Talk*

The aim and end result of the talk must be decided. The approach will vary depending on whether the trainer wishes to:

(i) Give general information of a subject

(ii) Gain acceptance for a new point of view

(iii) Change basic attitudes

(iv) Give detailed information

(v) Teach a particular skill

With a clearly defined purpose in mind, it will be easier to select appropriate material and to decide on the effective way to present it.

(c) *Time Available*

Making optimum use of the time available is an important consideration to be kept in mind by the trainer. A good trainer knows that it is better to have an audience still interested and wanting to know more after a short and fully used period than to have them tiered. Experience shows that 20 to 30 minutes is the maximum time a trainer can effectively speak continuously and receive the attention of the trainees. He should plan his talk so that interest is maintained by the use of examples, questions, humor, etc. Using humor for keeping the interest of the audience is advisable.

(d) *Subject Matter*

This is the main aspect of the lecture. Poor choice of subject or lack of sufficient knowledge can mean a total failure of the lecture. It is important for the trainer to speak from his experience but at the same time in keeping with the interest of the audience. The ideas for discussion or quiz programmes or student exercises should be recorded. It is better to give short lectures than a lengthy one. Further, the following basic structure can be followed.

(i) *Introduction:* An introduction about the subject matter can be brief and to the point presents the theme and objective of the talk. This should arouse the interest and curiosity of the audience right from the beginning. Opening remarks need to be planned and rehearsed with some care, because the first impression is going to be the best impression.

(ii) *Body of the talk:* The main theme of the talk should be developed in logical steps, so that the most important points will be remembered. One step should naturally start from the previous one, so that the audience is carried forward. Add examples related to the experience of the trainees, anecdotes and demonstrations to substantiate the points being made. Use visual aids to help the audience understand and remember what is important.

(iii) *Type of conclusion:* It will depend upon your objective but give a brief recapitulation in different words of the main points. The quality of the conclusion may determine whether the overall objective has been achieved.

Preparing the Lecture

The stages involved in preparing the lecture are as follows:

(a) *Draft the talk*

The trainer should prepare the notes from which he will speak. Whatever the type used (cards, paper sheets, etc) they should be easily readable and numbered to avoid confusions. Above all, notes should be notes and not a complete text. Check that the trainer is able to cover the material he has selected comfortably in the time available. Better to try it out on a friend or a tape recorder. Put approximate timings in the margin of the notes as guide.

(b) *Plan and prepare visual aids*

Various teaching aids may be employed to make the lecture more interesting and more understandable to the audience. Charts and graphs may make the quantitative data more meaningful. Photographs, drawings, and diagrams may classify the details of complex objects and structures. An outline of the main points will help the audience to remember the material.

(c) *Rehearse*

Rehearsing the lecture is an essential step even for experienced trainers. If a rehearsal audience can be recruited, the speaker has an opportunity to check his speech and his delivery. The chief value of rehearsal is in familiarizing the speaker with his speech. Even experienced trainers suffer from stage fright on occasions. One or two dry runs through a lecture can build a speaker's confidence in himself and in his material.

Delivering the Lecture

The written word can only be of a little help when it comes to advise on speaking technique. What is needed is practice followed by constructive criticism. Some of the essential points to be noted are as follows:

(a) *Setting the scene*

The trainer should arrive at the appointed place in time to check the arrangements like visual aids, etc. Physical arrangements such as layout of the chair, table, teaching aids, provision of chalk, and eraser should be checked.

(b) *Covering the material*

Start punctually. The trainer can speak from the notes, if necessary, but should not put the notes into them, read a phrase, pause and look at the audience. Leave sufficient time for questions at the end. Try to finish on time. If audience are asking questions close the meeting formally.

(c) *Posture*

The trainer should speak from a position that is comfortable for him but appropriate to the situation. It always better to stand and give lecture. If the group is small, he can sit around the small group.

(d) *Appearance*

He should be careful that there is nothing about their personal appearance, which is out of harmony with the occasion or which is likely to irritate the audience or distract their attention. The dress should be neat and suitable for the occasion.

(e) *Manner*

Any kind of leadership requires confidence and dignity to gain and hold the attention of the group. Be courteous. Careless choice of language or humor may create barriers to communication. Be sincere. The audience should not be misled by cleverness and they may not like insincerity. Be yourself — don't try to imitate anyone else. Be enthusiastic — let your talk reveal and convince the audience of your own interest in the subject. Establish eye-contact with the audience.

(f) *Gesture*

Any action or gesture must be natural and spontaneous. They should be purposeful and the mannerisms should be avoided. Because they may distract the attention of the audience.

(g) *Voice*

The tone of the voice can be altered to convey confidence, emotion, emphasis, and indignation. Pace and volume should be varied occasionally to avoid monotony.

(h) *Vocabulary*

It is better to use everyday language, avoiding slang, which could be misunderstood. Be careful with funny stories. Choose stories that are relevant to the point you are trying to make.

Advantages of Lecture Method

1. When the primary objective is to pass on information, the lecture method is very effective.
2. This method is useful if the number of trainees is large and teaching resources are scarce, and time available is short.

3. Lecturing is useful when basic theoretical knowledge has to be built up before practice or participative training is of any use.
4. When the important research findings are to be communicated, lecture method is convenient.

Disadvantages of Lecture Method

1. The spirit inquiry, which is the basis of learning, is prevented.
2. If the number is large, the advantage is disturbed.
3. It is not a suitable method for courses where people with work experience participate.
4. It produces monotony resulting in less absorption of knowledge.
5. Many times, lecturers are not aware of the taught process of the audience. This reduces the effectiveness of teaching because there is only one way of communication.
6. Flexibility with reference to inputs based on participants' reaction is low.
7. The lecture method is farthest from reality. The case method, problem solving exercises and action learning are nearer to reality and are more effective as training technique.

2. CASE STUDY METHOD

A case is a written description of a real decision-making situation in the organization or a situation that occurred in another organization. Managers are asked to study the case to determine the problems, analyze the problems for their significance, proposed solutions, choose the best solution, and implement it.

Definition

K.R. Andrews defines Case Study as "A written description of an actual situation in business, which provokes in the reader the need to decide what is going on, what the situation really is or what the problems are and what can and should be done".

A case study has a different meaning depending on how it is used. To some people, it will mean the same as a legal case, a precedent that can usefully be followed; to the researcher, a case may appear as a vehicle for testing hypotheses. We are concerned with the form of case study most suited to our objectives in management education. This form of case study will present the student with an authentic management problem. It will present reports, facts, and even opinions, but will not evaluate. The aim throughout is to train the student in analysis and decision-making. This aim is ensured by facing the student with a whole series of case situations designed to give him as wide an experience as possible.

Features of Case Study Method

1. The case study method is one of the important techniques of assisting in-service personnel in enhancing their efficiency and effectiveness at work by improving their professional knowledge, administrative skills and attitudes towards work and people.
2. A case depicts the actual process in the administrative situation, and represents slices of real life situations. It is a chronological narrative, which describes how one or more administrators had gone about the task of decision-making, and problem-solving in an administrative situation, enabling the reader to have a feel of the actual administrative situation.
3. The purpose of cases is to bring the reality of the administrative situation into the classroom and to help the trainees to learn from the concrete situations by detailed observation and analysis of available facts, rather than from assumptions.
4. In the case study approach, a number of cases belonging to different functional areas are discussed and in the process conceptual skills, analytical faculties and the art of making better decisions, after consideration of various alternatives and their implications, are developed in the trainees.

5. The practice of making detailed and accurate observations during the training by case study method will be carried into and used in the actual work situation for better evaluation of the situation, and for arriving at better decisions.
6. The method aids the trainees in blending their own practical experiences and theoretical reading, that must precede the case discussion, and in developing practical skills of problem-solving and decision-making.
7. In many real life situations, one is called upon to take decisions based on incomplete information and under conditions of uncertainty. The case method enables the trainees, now decision-makers, to take wise decisions, and to make plans for their successful implementation.
8. It helps them to develop their skills in discovering and defining the vital questions that need to be answered and then learn how to set about finding the answers.
9. The case method is based on the belief that the trainee can best attain managerial understanding and competence through the study, contemplation and discussion of actual situations.
10. It helps to develop habits of logical thinking and of searching for necessary information before reaching conclusions and making decisions based on them.
11. Case material, drawn from actual business situations and presented with only a minimum disguise, have a strong appeal to managers and the realism of the case material makes many managers relate what they are learning to their own situations. They use their own experience in analyzing the cases and derive management principles from the discussions of their analysis.
12. The case method is time consuming. The task of gathering all the facts, arranging them and then putting them into effective writing is a long process. Time is also required of the knowledgeable managers who supply the facts.
13. In addition to the time and talent involved, the actual use of the case method is time consuming as well. Because

general principles are derived from the detail of numerous specific instances, a large number of cases must be studied. This requires a lengthy programme, if real benefits are to be attained. Each session requires time for advance preparation as well as for group discussion of the case.

Advantages of Case Study

1. A case study presents a sample of business life, so that it may be studied in detail. Trainees learn to get most out of limited data by asking effective questions. They develop the habit of taking a greater number of factors into account than usual.
2. It helps the participants greater exposure to the experience and opinions of other trainees and kept them to realize that there are several ways of looking at, thinking about, and acting in a particular business situation. Thus, they are encouraged to develop flexibility in their approaches to organizational problems.
3. The method develops a systematic way of thinking about business issues and managerial decisions. Through examination and diagnosis of situations comparable to their own, participants may be drawn to re-examine their own attitudes and relationships.
4. In the course of studying and making decisions on a number of cases, participants will discover some of the underlying principles of management.
5. Using case studies is a convenient means of exposing participants to a diversity of business situations and problems during the training course.

In sum, the case study method accomplishes several objectives of management development programme, such as:

- It distributes knowledge and facts.
- It improves participant skills in problem analysis, communication, and decision-making.

- It affects attitude formation and particularly brings home to the participants that nothing is absolutely right or wrong in the field of human behaviour.

Types of Cases

1. The 'classic' Harvard approach uses very detailed case reports that may run to 40 to 50 pages of text, along with supporting charts and documents. The material is in the form of a running narrative. Anything and almost everything that might bear upon the situation is included. E.g., the history of the unit, biographies of key persons, information about location, environment, investment and finance, technology, product mix, byproducts if any, markets, inputs, profit and loss accounts, etc.
2. Another version of case method is 'short cases' running into only a page or two. All external information is removed leaving only the information relating to just one problem.
3. Another variation of case study is 'recordings of films' to present the case. The element of drama portrays the emotional overtones of any situation than is possible in the written version.
4. Another method is the 'incident process', in which the case is presented with only a necessary minimum of disguise. Here, problems come to the management's attention as incidents. The job of the manager is to decide what information is needed and then to find it.

Ways of using Cases

There are two ways of using cases. First, they can be used subsequent to the exposition of formal theory. In this way the trainees must apply their theory and knowledge to specific situations. Secondly, they must be assigned to the trainees for written analysis or oral class discussions without any prior explanation of the concepts and theory. The trainees are expected to derive useful generalizations and principles themselves. The second approach places heavy demands on the trainees, which requires that the trainees have good deal of maturity and background of the subject.

Case study method provides for learning by doing. Good cases are based upon real experiences and problem situations; therefore, the trainees' interest will be high. They are excellent for developing analytical thinking and problem-solving ability. Narrow-mindedness is reduced, because the trainees soon learn that others have studied the identical problem and come up with different solution. The case method is an excellent means of integrating the knowledge obtained from a number of disciplines.

The instructor using the case method must guard against:

(*a*) dominating the discussion

(b) permitting few people to dominate the discussion

(c) leading the discussion toward his or her preferred solution.

As a catalyst the instructor should encourage divergent view points, initiate discussion on points the trainees are missing and be thoroughly prepared.

Steps in Writing Case Study

In case writing or preparing case history, five steps are followed:

1. *Select type of problem and enterprise from which the material will be obtained*

   It is preferable to select an organization where the case writer is already known and accepted, particularly when it may be necessary to dig deep and obtain confidential material. It is of some interest to note that mature case writers learn more from problem situations in organizations other than their own.

2. *Observe and collect data objectively*

   During data collection process, one realizes that the facts may vary from situation to situation. Despite these, facts must be observed, recorded objectively, and as completely as the situation warrants. A good case is well documented and contains all information relevant to it.

3. *Write the case*

The primary criteria for writing the case are objectivity and practical usefulness. The length, structure, detail, method of presentation, literary standards, and style are secondary and should be subordinated to these twin primary criteria. Within the above, the following considerations will be useful.

(a) *Select the detail*— Before starting to write, re-evaluate the objectives in relation to the particular purpose.

(b) Decide if the material actually obtained incorporates multiple cases. If so, the cases should be separated out.

(c) *Set the scene quickly*— The first few sentences should enable the reader of the write-up to paint his own mental picture of the situation and envisage the type of problem involved.

(d) *Writ in the past sentence*— This is desirable if the case is likely to be used over a long period of time.

(e) *Decide the disguises*— To avoid embarrassments to the executives associated with the case and to the organization and to maintain confidentiality, these types of disguises are desirable.

4. *Clear the case*

Do review the write-up with the appropriate authorities in the organization from where you have drawn material for it. This examination will help to remove the commissions and omissions if any.

5. *Confirm the usefulness of the case*

This involves a full scale discussion of the case in realistic situations. For this purpose a trail with the members of the same organization is a good indicator but may be useful as an additional check point before its final use. At this stage, the following things must be observed:

(a) Correct the broad picture and understanding of the details of the situation.

(b) Data, which could be omitted without reducing the effectiveness of the case or alternatively, additional data that needs to be added.

(c) Subject matter pertaining to the case.

(d) Improved methods of its presentation in respect of time, audio-visuals, charts, and diagrams.

(e) Prepare leaders' note. Preferably, the leader should be the same person as the case writer but this is not always possible, more so, if the case has wider utility elsewhere and in other similar situations.

Variables that Decide the Success or Failure of Case Study

There are three variables, which decide the success or failure of case study, which are as follows:

1. *The case itself:* It must be reach in facts, as close to reality as possible, be well narrated, have some dramatic effect and carefully chosen cut-off points.
2. *The participants:* The more experienced the participants are, the more they will get out of a good case.
3. *The leader/conductor/trainer:* He must respect the participants, restrict himself to generating productive discussion and to act as a catalyst. A good leader is non-directive, usually has no ready-made answers and his approach is that of a learner himself in a democratic set-up.

Through the case study one learns many things as follows:

1. The process of analysis
2. The art of marshaling the facts
3. The skill of separating chaff from the grain
4. Identifying the problems
5. Picking out the problems that need priority in decision-making

6. Looking at the alternatives available for action
7. Weighing the alternatives and their consequences
8. Choosing the right alternative in making a good decision

Limitations of Case Study

1. Personal bias—A trainee's thinking is inevitably colored and limited by prejudices and pre-occupations of which he may not aware.
2. The second limitation of case study is it calls for skill with language. Many trainees are sent to case study courses because they lack communication skills. But much of the work in analyzing cases can be done through group discussions.

3. BUSINESS GAMES

Business game is one of the important training techniques available to us and it is a powerful instrument. It is also a logical step in the development of teaching techniques. Business game concentrates on management principles such as planning, decision-making and effective utilization of time, men, and material. Some games aim at teaching specific skills and techniques, particularly those games which are built around production, marketing and financial functions. Games can be incorporated into training in many ways. They can be used at the beginning of training courses as an orientation devise. They can be used more than once, before and after a particular management principle or technique has been discussed.

Definition

ILO - "This is a training technique in which participants grouped into teams considered a sequence of problems and organize themselves to make decisions. It is a form of simulation, which may be defined as a sequential decision making exercises structured around a hypothetical model of an organization's operations, in which participants assume roles in managing the simulated operations. Its most crucial aspect is the attempt to reproduce the social, psychological and economic dynamics of organizational behaviour in an artificial setting".

"A management game is classroom simulation exercise in which teams of students compete against each other or against an environment to achieve given objectives".

Management games describe the operating characteristics of a company, industry, or enterprise. In a typical computerized management game procedure, the team players are asked to make a series of operating decisions. In one game, for example, the players are asked to decide on such matters as the price of the product, purchase of materials, products scheduling, funds, marketing, etc. When each player on the team has made a decision, the interactions of these decisions are computed (manually or by computer) in accordance with the model. Players on the team first reconcile their individual decisions with those of the other team members prior to making a final decision. Then each team's decision is compared with other teams. The result of that team's profit, market share, and so forth is compared and a winner or best team performance is determined.

Purposes of Games

The purpose of management games is to increase a person's understanding of:

1. Specific organizational problems (production, marketing, etc.)
2. Inter-relatedness of the functions and parts of an organization and its relation to its environment.
3. Problems of organization's policy and decision-making.
4. Problems of working in a team.

Features of Games

1. General management games do not teach anything very specific about the business enterprise or the management of the firm. However, they may serve to demonstrate

broad facts of organizational life such as, the areas of an enterprise or that they have to be coordinated.

2. Games may make a functional executive more tolerant of his co-workers in other department and aware those problems.
3. The emotional impact of game probably makes it a suitable technique for changing attitudes, provided the game situation is sufficiently clear to pinpoint the attitude to be changed.
4. It does not provide experience in learning from experience, particularly in the application of statistical and analytical methods.
5. Games provoke interest which may lead the participants to additional reading and study. They may change the attitudes and they seem to give a feel for organizational problems.

Types of Games

Games can be classified on the basis of coverage, competitive element and processing of results.

1. *Coverage*

(a) *Total enterprise game:* Such games link different functions like marketing, inventory etc, in a simulated company to show how these functions are inter-related. This has to be kept in mind while taking decisions.

(b) *Functional games:* Such games cover only a specific function in the simulated company. Trainees will learn about problems in functions like sales. This game could as well be advertising vis-à-vis increase in sales.

(c) *Other specialist areas:* Games have been designed to test out impact of different public policies of the government.

2. *Competitive element*

(a) *Interacting game:* Here the results are affected not only by the decisions of the team but also by the decisions of the competitors.

(b) *Non-interacting game:* Here each individual team is in command of its own performance. The competition continues, but results are dependent on the team and its actions and not on the decisions taken by any competing team.

3. *Processing of results*

(a) *Computer game:* Computation of data in complex games becomes difficult. Such games require computers to process data and give feedback.

(b) *Non-computer game:* In less complex games computation work can be done either by manually or by simple calculators.

A typical top management type game consists of three teams, each representing a company, which competes in producing and selling the same product in the same market. Each company tries to achieve a good financial position, to increase its assets, to make a good return on investment, and to place itself in a strong position. Each team or company makes quarterly decisions in regard to product price, advertising, product volume and cost, research and development expenditure, and investment in additional plant. These decisions are fed into computer that has been programmed with a mathematical model that simulates a typical economic situation in the market. The computer then, feeds back to each team its own performance data derived from the interaction with other competing teams. Teams can change their strategies as the game progresses and determine the impact upon performance of such changes. A game contains many variables present in real life business. The trainees can learn the consequences of their decision in a classroom situation, which is a low risk environment. Students play different roles in their teams and they learn how to work together cooperatively. A game takes the learning situation a step further than can be done in a case study.

Advantages of Games

The advantages of games include the integration of several interacting decisions, the ability to experiment with decisions, the provision of feedback experiences on decisions, and the requirement that decisions be made with inadequate data, which usually simulates reality.

1. They are able to demonstrate broad and vital facts of organizational life. One such example is that different functions in an organization are inter-related and managers should take a systematic approach of management rather than a sectarian function based approach.
2. It helps in changing attitudes. For example, the participant becomes more tolerant to his colleague of other departments.
3. It provides experience in the application of statistical and analytical methods.
4. Games are quite absorbing, provoking, interests in participants.

Steps in Running a Business Game

1. *Briefing the group:* Enough time should be spent in briefing the participants. The trainer should read out instructions slowly and carefully encouraging the participants to clarify doubts by asking questions.
2. *First run by participants:* Enough time should be devoted for the first run as it takes some time to familiarize with new situation.
3. *First feedback:* The trainer should quickly finish all calculations and give the feedback to maintain the tempo. It is advisable to keep all necessary charts, ready reckoner to finish the calculations quickly.

4. *Publication of information on results achieved:* There may be some delay in the publication of certain information to reproduce the real life circumstances. This will not only encourage competition but will also test how well participants handle and interpret data.
5. *Repeat rounds:* The participants should be encouraged to strict to the time schedule. Every managerial decision has a time dimension and they should be encouraged to inculcate the merits of timely decision.
6. *End of game:* No advance warning of the end should be given to the participants. The trainer should announce the end of the game as final results are returned to the participants.
7. *Evaluation:* The trainer should bring out the lesions learned. The evaluation should never be hurried. If time is short, savings should be made on the actual running of the game rather than on the evaluation.

Trainer's Role

A trainer has to be active and fully involve to produce desired results from this method. He should also be prepared to answer some of the unexpected questions. He should keep the following points in mind:

1. He should have complete understanding of the games. It is advisable to have a trial run with few friends in case it is the first time that the trainer is running the game.
2. He should clearly explain the game to the participants.
3. He should be always alert to handle new situations while running the game.
4. He should give the feedback quickly.
5. He should plan conducting the game carefully to avoid dull moments.
6. He should have the complete situation under his control. This can come only by practice. It is for this reason that trial run is advisable whenever the trainer attempts new game.

7. In the evaluation session the trainer should steer the discussion into productive channels of learning.
8. He should avoid declaring any body as a winner. The winner is one who learnt the game fully.
9. The game must be compared with real life situations.
10. The real evaluation that the trainer has to do is to determine whether the objectives were met or not.

Limitations of Games

1. There is a tendency to devote too much time to play and not enough to a careful analysis and critic of the games results. Many suggest that games should be used in conjunction with more conventional teaching devices like lectures and discussions.
2. The way in which the teams are organized has a limitation. Keeping groups together simply because they have worked together does not enhance what they get from the experience.
3. Many management games involve only quantitative variables and ignore human elements of organization completely.

4. ROLE PLAY

Role play is one of the important tools of management which has greater relevance to today's training programmes. It is an educational technique in which some problem involving human interactions, real or imaginary, is presented, then spontaneously acted out.

Definition

"Asking some one to imagine that they are either themselves or another person in a particular situation. The situation may be defined in space and time, and by information, resources, constraints and social or political or industrial environment. They are asked to perform tasks in that situation and to deal with circumstances which arise".

ILO - "Role playing is a training technique in which participants assume an identity other than their own, to cope with real or hypothetical problems in human relations and other areas. Role lifting and role taking are other terms used to describe this process".

In role play the participant is asked to behave as they would be in a certain situation and in a certain role. They may be observers who will join in the debriefing and learn from their own observation. Role play is the experiencing of a problem by the role player under a particular set of circumstances so that their own ideas emerge and they develop understanding or skills.

Major Aims

1. Role play allows a player to practice reacting in conflict and other stressful situations.
2. Roles can be selected which are in contrast to the real life situation of the player so as to provide various experience and widen the insight of the trainee into the real meaning and possible implication of the behaviour of other persons.
3. In addition to the general insight into human interactions made possible by the activity, the trainees can be helped to modify their own behaviour patterns by getting feedback from others who have watched his play a role.

Methodology of Role Play

Two approaches are generally used viz., structured role playing and spontaneous role playing.

Structured role playing: here a leader selects both the situation and the roles to be enacted and specifies the goals of the activity. This type of pre-planned role playing provides very elaborate written materials that describe the roles and situation and elicit complex responses from the observers. A variation of this approach consists of having the role playing planned in advance by members of the group itself rather than by the leader. This would be appropriate when trying to communicate information, setting and studying a social problem or interpreting a report. The leader or group planning the exercise may determine the degree of spontaneity desired and adjust the situation.

Spontaneous role play: This approach relies on the problem situation arising from the group discussion, without advance planning by the group or the leader. Here the enactment serves as the briefing to the group on the problem and situation.

Both structured and spontaneous role playing relate to learning through:

(*a*) doing;

(*b*) imitation;

(*c*) observation and feedback;

(*d*) analysis.

Advantages of Role Play

1. Role play provides an opportunity for developing insight into what is happening, when it is happening.
2. Role playing emphasizes the importance that feelings and emotions play in any problems, especially problems associated with human relations.
3. Role playing enables the manager or supervisor to see a situation from a perspective different to his own.
4. Role playing develops the interests of the learner, thereby providing a situation during the course of which attitudes can be modified and new attitudes develop.

Unique Values of Role Play

1. It requires the person to carry out a decision he may have reached.
2. It permits the practice of carrying an action and makes it clear that good human relations require skill.
3. It trains a person to be aware of and sensitive to the feelings of others.

4. Each person is able to discover his own personal fault.
5. It permits training in the control of feelings and emotions.

Uses of Role Play

1. It is used to describe or demonstrate a skill.
2. It helps to practice a procedure or skill.
3. Through it we can learn how people behave in a situation.
4. It develops a sensitivity to human emotions and feelings.
5. It provides a stimulant to creativity.

Learning Theory and Role Play

Malcolm Show has invented four kinds of learning that can take place through role play:

1. Learning by practice of a desired skill
2. Learning through imitation
3. Learning through observations and feedback
4. Learning through analysis and conceptualization.

Strength and Weakness of Role Play

Strength

1. It is motivational and effective because it involves activity
2. It closes the gap between training and real life situations.
3. It is more likely to change the attitudes.
4. It gives practice in various types of behaviour.
5. It provides good feedback for both the trainer and the trainee.
6. It permits training in the control of feelings and emotions.
7. It is trainee-centered and addresses the needs of the trainees.
8. It portrays work problems and dynamics of group interaction.

Weaknesses

1. The trainer may loose control over what is learnt and the order in which it is learnt.

2. Simplifications can mislead.
3. It takes lot of time.
4. The effectiveness depends on the quality of the trainer and trainee.
5. It may be seen as two entertaining.
6. The learning may depend on what students already know. They may introduce misleading information.

Preparation

The initial stages of using role play are the same as preparing for any other teaching task. But the stages are more critical than the classroom situation. The first step in preparation is to decide on the teaching objectives. Secondly, to clarify the position of the role play in the overall training programme. Thirdly, the trainer has to keep in mind the constraints. Fourthly, the trainer should write his own role plays.

Writing the Role Play

The first stage is the preparation of a general scenario. It helps at this stage to consider the key actions of the participants and the result to be achieved. Characteristics to be considered are as follows:

1. *Characters:* The key characters must be decided.
2. *Time:* Past, present or future.
3. *Reality:* The closeness of the role play to correspond to real facts.
4. *Personalisation:* Whether the characters are real or known people or symbolic.
5. *Size:* The numbers and grouping of roles.
6. *Length of time:* Slow or fast.
7. *Information:* How will information be presented to participants during the role play.
8. *Role allocation:* By chance or by design. By design means handling of sex, age, etc.

Key Features of Individual Roles

1. Physical attributes (age, sex).
2. Personality traits (relevance to the role play).
3. Surrounding circumstances, status, authority, constraints, power.
4. Their skills and abilities.
5. How much they know.
6. What they believe, social expectations.
7. Their objectives, motives and targets.

Steps in Role Play Process

1. *Warm-up:* Structured role play requires more planning than spontaneous role play. The objective of the warm-up is to get the trainees participate in a constructive manner. The trainer's introduction to the session should be such that it should create interest.
2. *Enactment:* Before conducting the role play, the trainer should carry out the following things — Read loud the general information, Giving briefing sheets to the players.
3. *Post-enactment discussion:* Reactions to the role play should be obtained first from the participants then from the audience.
4. *Techniques:* The following techniques can be adopted.

   (a) Fishbowl — In the middle with observers around

   (b) Multiple — Two or three simultaneously

   (c) Role rotation — Give another person a chance to play the role

   (d) Role reversal — Switch roles between two players

   (e) Supporter — A volunteer from the observers speech for the role player

(f)	Alter ego/doubling	— An extra player reveals the feelings of the role player
(g)	Consultant group	— Groups who give advice
(h)	Mirroring	— Re-enact in front of original players
(i)	Replay	— With modified format
(j)	Chair	— Using an object to speak
(k)	Silent auxiliary	— Speaks to another person
(l)	Positioning	— Rearrange furniture and players

Problems during Role Play

1. *Player departs from the role:* Sometimes the players may depart from their role.
2. *Poor performance:* we cannot expect good performance from all.
3. *Lack of insight:* one should understand the importance of the particular role.
4. *Emotions:* the trainer may not have control in which the role play goes.
5. Not taking the role play seriously.
6. *Repetition:* Due to boredom repetition may arise.

Role of the Trainer

The trainer must act as adjudicator, control the time and correct any problems. It is not the duty of the trainer to act as a therapist and he should avoid getting into personal or emotional matters. Unwanted learning must be avoided.

Debriefing

A great deal of learning takes place during debriefing. A role play without a systematic, logical and well conducted debriefing session is not useful. A three phase scheme can be used as follows:

Phase 1

Clearing up the role play: The purpose of this phase is to bring the players out of the role and relieve the tension or anxiety. It is also an opportunity to correct mistakes, establish facts and clear up mis-understanding.

Phase 2

Drawing conclusions: Under this phase, the trainer establishes sequences, causes and effects. It is also an opportunity for the players to develop self observation and observational skills. The aim of the trainer should be to draw generalized conclusions, conclusions about the way in which people behave, analyses the causes of behaviour and decide on to improve the situation.

Phase 3

Develop an action plan: In order to avoid the role play being an isolated one from the real teaching and learning, it is important to arrange the ways to continue the process within the overall training plan. For this purpose the trainer can follow-up with a repeat of the role play, organize students into action groups, get the students to commit themselves to actions and write-up plans, agree criteria for success and put a time scale for action.

The key to the good debriefing is to allow sufficient time, to ensure that each person has opportunity to speak and to understand everyone's feelings.

Drawbacks of Role Play

1. Much of its effectiveness depends on the skill of the leader.
2. Role playing is time consuming and necessarily restricts the number and complexity of problems that can be dealt with at one time.
3. Many feel that it is artificial, resulting in little transfer of behaviour change to real situations, and the theatricality that makes it engrossing for participants may lead them to forget the problems they are suppose to deal with.

Training experiences of Case Study and Role Play — A Comparison

Case Study	Role Play
1. Presents a problem for discussion	1. Places a problem in a life like setting
2. The problem is decided from previous events	2. The problem involves ongoing processes
3. The problem involves others	3. The problem involves the participants
4. Emphasises the importance of facts	4. Emphasises the importance of feelings
5. Facilitates intellectual involvement	5. Makes for emotional involvement
6. Trains in the exercise of judgment	6. Trains in emotional control
7. Consequences of action are undermined	7. Allows continuous feedback.
8. Deals with emotional and attitudinal aspects in an intellectual frame of reference	8. Deals with emotional and attitudinal aspects in an experiential frame of reference

4. On the other hand if the problems used lack sufficient conflict or variety, participants may find it boring.
5. The important thing is the place of spontaneity in the culture of community or group concerned. It is much more likely to be successful if the group is accustomed to informal, game like atmosphere required.

5. IN-BASKET EXERCISE

The name is derived from the famous IN and OUT trays found on the table of an executive. These trays are more important in the offices of government and companies.

Definition

ILO "The In-Basket is a simulation of a managers work load on a typical day. The name is derived from the wire baskets that formally were seen on almost every manager's desk, marked IN and OUT for mail and memoranda".

Aims of In-Basket Exercise

1. The exercise provides information on how a participant handles a sequence of problems in a given situation, under some pressure and thus, some measure of his potential or his competency.
2. As a training device, it is used to help the trainees identify areas in planning, organizing, and administrative behaviour in which their skills need to be improved, as well as an opportunity to practice those skills in a situation in which he can obtain feedback on his performance.

Divisions of In-Basket Exercise

1. A set of instructions to the player — This sets the background, tells him what the circumstances are, an organization structure, where this is necessary and all other items necessary to set the stage and put him in the position as nearly as possible of a man arriving at work and sitting down for the day's work.

2. The contents of the In-Basket — Each of these is in a separate sheet, some parts are handwritten, some are inter office memos and others are letters from outside the organization.
3. Notes for the guidance of the instructor.

The first two of these sections are designed for reproduction, so that each player has his own full set of both. The third is not for distribution at all and it is for the guidance of the trainer.

Methodology

The participant is required to assume the role of a manager in a hypothetical organization. He then, is presented with a number of problems. These problems are presented to the manager in the form of letters, memos, and all put in IN-tray of the participant. The problems could be in any field of management. The participant is asked to read the papers in the IN-tray and take appropriate action within a limited time.

The participants' role does not end with suggesting solutions. He has to take action as has to be done by a manager in the real life. He has to write notes and memos to complete the exercise. At the end of the exercise, there will be a written record of every action, which each participant has taken.

Advantages

1. The major advantage of this method is that it is rooted in the real life situation of the corporate world.
2. It enhances the skills in decision-making and problem-solving.
3. This exercise can be designed to focus on the activities that are part of all managerial positions. It can also be designed to insist certain specific acts of performance.
4. This exercise can be altered to suit the level of a trainee. This game can use materials relevant to each training.
5. This method has been advantageous in assessing specific dimensions like written communication skills, sensitivity,

risk taking, initiative, planning and organizing, management control, use of delegation, problem analysis, and decision-making.

Trainer's Role

The trainer can easily construct In-Basket exercises by going through the relevant files of the company. This approach will give an impression of realism. Other trainers can also construct such exercises from their experiences mixed with imagination. But the content of the basket should look real.

The trainer should explain to the group—what an In-Basket exercise is? Then he distributes the instructions to the participants. Time must be allowed to be read for reinforcement and to ask questions. In some cases, the trainer will have to decide on his own as to what additional instructions should be given. Then, the trainer should distribute the contents of the In-Basket, one set to each participant. Fix a time limit considering the exercise and profile of the group. The time limit should not be extended. Then, the group should be allowed to discuss. The trainer should act as a facilitator for the group discussion. What is important is that the participants are able to logically argue about their decision and see where they went wrong. In this way, a participant learns different approaches to solve a problem.

6. EXPERIMENTAL LEARNING TECHNIQUES

Experimental learning technique is an action oriented behaviour situation. The purpose of the action situation is to have participants generate their own data about each of the key concepts to be studied or understood. Observation is important criteria in making this programme a success. When a group starts to examine its experiences the trainer is in a position to help in this process. His responsibilities in focusing learning and making it clear for each participant are extremely important. The primary duty of a trainer is as follows:

1. Drawing out the data from the participants in terms of what has actually happened together with their feelings about it.

2. Helping the participants to see the cause and effect of the actions of the people, i.e., initiating the behaviour of a person and the type of response he receives to it.
3. Relating the classroom experience to what happens in on-the-job in the organization situations.

Experimental learning techniques have the following methods.

1. *Sensitivity training*

It aims at developing sensitivity within people towards thoughts, feelings, and behaviour of other persons and through this, improve upon once human interactions. One basic thing relating to this approach is that it is voluntary. Being an emotional experience, the degree of change depends upon the level of emotional involvement. It provides an opportunity to experience some concepts of management just as a manager experiences them in his organizational situation. Experimental learning with its action-oriented behaviour situation allows to understand and analyze key management concepts. This is group training. This is a group training method that uses intensive participation and immediate feedback for self-analysis and change. The benefits of sensitivity training are as follows:

- *(a)* Participants remain involved and enthusiastic.
- *(b)* As the responsibility for the learning experience lies with the participant, he will make positive efforts to derive as much possible from the exercise.
- *(c)* Sensitivity training attempts to develop the diagnostic ability of the participants — the ability to perceive reality. The individual is made to aware of himself and his impact on others.
- *(d)* It increases sensitivity and awareness towards others and their styles. It helps in understanding how conflicts arise and are resolved.

The major problem of sensitivity training is the effectiveness, is the transfer problem, i.e. the inability of the participant to apply concepts and awareness gained in the laboratory or group to his job.

Role of the trainer — The trainer is responsible for creating an environment with time and space barriers. He should focus the discussion and group learning for constructive purposes. He is a facilitator who helps participants see cause-effect relationship of individual actions on others and relate the laboratory experience to what happens in organizations on the job.

2. *T–Groups*

The T–group system was developed in USA where a training laboratory was held to impart the skills of a change agent. To be change agent, it was considered necessary to understand the behavioural pattern of variety of skills and experiences — self awareness, inter-personal relationships, team work, group and organizational process, and inter-group conflict resolution. Change, however, remains the key word in any form of sensitivity training — change towards greater trust and openness in attitude. T–groups lead to understand the self and contribute towards organizational change through training in attitude change in the participants and creating better team work.

Classification of T – groups

(a) *Stranger groups:* Participants in this group have no prior knowledge of one another. The advantage of such group is that members can express and involve themselves without fear or retaliation.

(b) *Family groups:* Participants in this group belong to the same department and have prior knowledge of one another.

(c) *Cousin groups:* Persons of this group are from the same organization or institution but not in the same department. They are quite independent of each other.

A T–group may consist of eight to fifteen persons. The trainer after setting the objectives of the T–group gets back creating a vacuum, which allows the participants to develop structure and meaning for themselves. Data developed by the group behaviour is used to understand the "here-and-now". Analysis is direct and immediate to see through the reality from perceptions. T–group process concentrates on the present to the total exclusion of the past and the participants are in the act of observing while participating. There is no prescribed agenda and the conventional forms of trainer-trainee interactions are avoided. Instead, the trainer serves to facilitate the group cohesiveness achieve a collective atmosphere and provide psychological security.

While imparting feedback in T–group, the following points must be considered:

(a) It must be honest.

(b) State the behavioural terms.

(c) Keep it timely, immediate, and direct.

(d) Feedback should be based on the behaviour exhibited within the group, not on assumptions and past knowledge.

(e) It should be constructive, not with the sole intention to criticize.

3. *Transactional Analysis*

This exercise is based on a psychological theory called transactional analysis developed by Eric Berne. A transaction is an exchange between two people, where one says or does something and the other responds. According to Berne, all of us have one of three operating ego states — parent, adult, and child at any time. It recognizes that no matter how old we are there are within each one of us three different modes of being:

The Child Reacting spontaneously, instinctively, and emotionally to any experience. The child is sometimes free and joyful, sometimes submissive, fearful or stubborn.

The parent Conditioned by the training we received from the childhood from our parents and other authority figures, to react from a sense of obligation and duty. The parent is sometimes caring and understanding, sometimes harsh and critical.

The adult Making independent judgments, looking for reasons, seeking alternative solutions in difficult situations.

Each of us react to different situations, sometimes as a child, sometimes as a parent, and sometimes as an adult, and the way we react often brings out the opposite reaction in the other person. Each of these modes are appropriate at certain times and inappropriate at others. Each has both positive and negative forms.

Transactional Analysis (TA) was originally used to refer to the analysis of transactions or interactions between people. Such analysis used Berne's original concept of ego states as observable phenomena. TA is both a theory of human personality and a system for the improvement of human relations. Its application to organizations provide a systematic approach to understand the links between human needs and behaviours and the ways the organizations are effective or ineffective in solving their problems and serving their customers. An analyst can offer guidance on ways to create healthy organizational cultures in which individuals can functions effectively, creatively, and enthusiastically.

A transaction is a basic unit of social interaction. It consists of exchange of words and behaviour between two people. The heart of TA is the study and diagramming of the exchanges between two people. In this analysis the learner identifies the ego state that both the initiator and the respondent exhibit in the transaction.

Courses on TA are given to managers and professionals to help them improve inter-personal communications and effectiveness. The key beliefs of TA are as follows:

(*a*) All people are OK as human beings, even though their behaviour may be unacceptable.

(*b*) People have an urge to grow and develop themselves even though they may be repressing this without being aware of it.

(*c*) We make decisions and therefore, responsible for our behaviour. A function of TA is to help understand this and make fresh decisions where our old choices are leading to current problems.

The aim of using TA is to create more autonomy, which Berne described as claiming yourself, owning yourself, and deciding on your own destiny. He suggests three elements to autonomy.

- *Spontaneity:* Being free to choose what to do and having many options.
- *Intimacy:* Able to be open, close and trusting.
- *Awareness:* Knowing what is happening now.

The primary concepts in TA are ego states, transactions, strokes, and ways people spend their time.

With regard to ego states, there are three ego states — parent, adult, and child. The parent ego state of a person comprises the judgmental, value-laden, rule-making and moralizing component of personality. It is expressed by advise, admonitions, and do's and don'ts. The adult ego state is authentic, direct, and reality based. It is rational, fact-seeking, thinking, problem-solving. The child ego state constitutes the emotional, creative, spontaneous, and impulsive component of personality. It must be noted that ego states are not tied to one's age. In the course of daily interactions adults are likely to display all there ego states, however, one state may predominate.

Contracting: Key to TA Effectiveness

There is a significant principle arises from the assumptions of TA, which is practiced as part of contractual arrangement. Contracts may be written or verbal, the main point is that we discuss and agree why we are interacting when we plan to use to help someone grow. In the case of organizational work, there are three parties to a contract — trainer, participant, and the organization. The rights and responsibilities of all parties must be respected and balanced. The contract contains the following:

1. *Procedural:* Administrative details, such as when to meet, where, how, and who keeps notes, etc.
2. *Professional:* What the trainer offers as a professional trainer, consultant, mentor, etc.
3. *Psychological:* What will happen outside our awareness?

Stroke

Stroke is a TA term for a unit of recognition. Any interaction with others is therefore and exchange of strokes. The recognition can be positive or negative. Strokes are probably the secret of universe. We all have a biological need to interact with other human beings. Without such contacts we fail to develop ourselves. We all learn as children that we can stimulate negative strokes more easily than positively. Strokes are a biological necessity and we will settle for negatives rather than being ignored. When an individual goes to another organization, it will take some time to recreate adequate stroking patterns in areas such as new manager, new colleagues, new procedures, new customers, etc. The new team may have well established stroking patterns between themselves and need time to incorporate the new comer.

Ways People Spend Their Time

These are classified into six categories, namely withdrawal, rituals, activities, past times, psychological games, and authentic encounters or intimacy.

Through TA, by exposing their managerial personnel to these courses, top managers hope to improve their self understanding, interpersonal effectiveness, communication, and leadership skills. TA generates less tension in the learner and it is less threatening to him than in sensitivity training.

T.A. can help us to eradicate the dysfunctional aspect of our personality. Behaviour being a reflection of one's personality, it will provide valuable insights to know one's personality. Dysfunctional aspects of one's personality develop from our cultural assumptions developed during childhood, the ways in which we are supposed to control and the way in which we have to deal with our feelings. This method involves the sharing of concepts and knowledge of T.A., playing structured exercises and games leading the participants to look at themselves and their behaviour.

The primary duty of the trainer is to interpret the group behaviour in terms of ego states in which the participants are operating in the here-and-now situation.

4. *Fish Bowl Exercise*

It involves the active participation of the trainees to enhance their learning experience. It is used in providing skills in understanding human behaviour. It effectively uses group interaction to develop in the participants a degree of self-awareness.

Objectives of fish bowl exercise

(a) To inculcate the participants the discipline of observing others and provide objective and constructive feedback.

(b) To learn about one self, one's behaviour and personality as seen through the eyes of others.

(c) The aspects to which the fish bowl exercise can be put to uses are — individual and group behaviour, communication, roles individuals play in group, content of communication, etc.

Method of conducting the exercise

The exercise can involve up to 25 participants seated in two concentric circles (one inner, the other outer). The inner circle is the target group, the outer group is asked to comment on the content and group process of the inner group members. The trainer should select a topic for discussion that is either familiar to the participants or of interest to them. Participants can then identify with the topic and generate a discussion. The feedback must be provided after the discussions are over. The feedback must never be critical or it loses its constructive nature. After one cycle of the exercise is completed, the outer group will change places with the inner group and become the target group. The inner group members become observers and the exercise is repeated.

7. IT RELATED TRAINING

I. Web-based training

The internet and the World Wide Web have captured the attention of trainers around the world. The internet is neither a company, a software system, nor a service. It is not owned by anyone. It is simply a generic name given to the global network of computer networks and it enables information to be passed around even when one network is out of action.

Benefits of web-based training

1. *Reduced training cost per head:* The cost of using an interactive web programme is less than traditional methods. While it is expensive to develop interactive programmes, delivery cost per course is lower per trainee.
2. *Learning gains:* It increases the learners' understanding of the course material. It combines the best of self-paced, self study training with the classroom training.
3. *Consistency of presentation:* The course material is presented in the same way to the same standard every time.
4. *Up to date material:* The course material can be updated on the web server with any curriculum changes. The new material will be available quicker.
5. *Timeliness of information delivery:* Using web, test results can be delivered to the trainees within seconds of completion, providing quick feedback.
6. *Faster completion of training:* A trainee can work at a pace that suits him best as well as bypassing the training that is not relevant.

7. *Content retention:* Because of the interactive nature of the presentation, combining multimedia, enables the development of courses that stimulate real life situations and provide immediate feedback.
8. *Better utilization of trainers:* The best trainers are used for training and their best is utilized.
9. *Affordable technology:* Web will not require any new expenditure on new hardware or software. Most people have access to a computer, a modem, and access to a telephone.
10. *Control over course management:* One can limit or extend training opportunities to any small or large group of trainces. The trainer can also track the trainees' progress promptly.
11. *Training more accessible:* The internet has opened up new field of training opportunities for anyone who wants to learn.

Drawbacks of this system

1. *New software and procedures:* Trainees will need to become familiar with web browser software and using the internet.
2. *Bandwidth/browser limitations:* Limitations in bandwidth may restrict instructional methodologies.

II. Computer-based training (CBT)

Computer-based training programmes have the following advantages over traditional methods of training:

1. When large numbers of trainees are to be trained, it is a good system.
2. When widely dispersed workforce is to be trained.
3. When we need to promote a standard message.
4. To reduce the costs of training to a large number of people.

5. It benefits employers and employees — CBT programmes can be used out of working hours and will not involve any travel.
6. To preserve a unique or rare piece of information or skill.

Development of CBT

The main standards of CBT are:

1. CBT on mainframe: This was the first manifestation of the genre and made its appearance 30 years back.
2. CBT on floppy disk
3. Multimedia based courseware: Typically on CD-ROM.
4. Interactive video: Contained on laser disk and requiring a laser disk player as well as a PC in order to run the course.
5. CD-I (Compact Dist Interactive)
6. Networked courseware

Issues relating to CBT usage

1. The introduction of CBT will not mean the end of in-house stand up trainers. Trainers need to have explained to them how the technology can be complement the service they provide.
2. Users need to be shown and must understand that self-paced learning is effective.
3. The management must feel it that it is a more convenient and cost-effective method of training.
4. Those who are purchasing the programmes must have confidence in the technology and be prepared to invest in machines that have multimedia capabilities and in the courseware that will meet staff development needs.

The staff must be computer literate; otherwise, a course must be conducted for them.

8. PROGRAMMED LEARNING

Programmed learning (PL) is called as programmed instruction also. This is one of the innovative methods of teaching introduced in management training. The materials to be learned are prepared in such a way that it can be presented to the trainees in series of sequential steps. These steps progress from simple to more complex levels of instruction. The information to be taught is known as a *programme*. The person who writes the programme is called as programme writer or programmer. The trainees to whom the programme is written are called as *target population*.

Definition

ILO defines PL as - PL is a method whereby the trainee teaches himself by working through a series of steps all leading to carefully defined goals or objectives. He cannot go on to the next step until he has mastered the preceding one and so on to the end. To ensure that he is really learning the information in each step, he must answer questions correctly. He has immediate knowledge of results at each step so that he can check to see how well he is doing.

Features of PL

1. Trainees learn at their own pace.
2. Trainers are not a key part of learning.
3. The material to be learned is broken down into small units or stages.
4. Each step logically builds upon those that have preceded it.
5. The trainee is given immediate knowledge of results for each answer he gives.
6. There is active participation by the trainee at each step in the programme.

Forms of PL

There are three types of PL, as follows:

1. *Linear Programming:* This method was developed by Skinner. Under this method the trainee works through all the sequences of a book in straight path from the first page to the last. He is given feedback at every step.

2. *Intrinsic Programming:* This form developed by Dr. Crowder, makes the trainee work through the programme by one of several paths or branches according to the responses he chooses. Since the learners' choice of reply determines which path of learning he would take through the programme, this form of programming is known as intrinsic.
3. *Adaptive Programming:* This was developed by Gordon Pask. According to this the programmes can only be presented in machines, which adapt to the trainees. This form makes allowance for more variations in the study ability.

Differences between PL and other methods

1. PL is self-instructional. Other methods depend greatly on a trainer or facilitator.
2. The subject matter is carefully analyzed and each unit is designed to meet specified objectives.
3. Trainees are required to take part actively and receive immediate feedback. In other methods, it is difficult to give immediate feedback to the trainees.
4. Programmes are thoroughly tasted. This avoids problems associated with inexperience trainers.

Masters Each Step

The success of PL depends on the success at each step or mastery of each piece of information. Such steps are as follows.

1. *Reasonably-sized steps:* The information is put into reasonable steps according to the type of material and the level of the particular group for whom the programme is written. The steps must be correctly tailored to the ability of the trainees.
2. *Prompts:* Putting the information into reasonable steps may not be sufficient to obtain correct response, so prompts or hints are used. The types of hints are pictorial, sequential, thematic, and grammatical prompts.

3. *Testing:* In PL, a good programme is thoroughly tested before it is printed by a large number.
4. *Immediate feedback:* Each step must be provided with the feedback. The principle of feedback is — stimulus (information + question), trainee, response, and feedback.

Motivation

Motivation is the desire to learn or the desire to acquire certain skills. The object of PL is to maximize this desire to learn. This is achieved in large part by knowledge of results (feedback), which encourages the trainee. It is generally agreed that knowledge of results plays a major part in motivating trainees to work through programmes.

In summary, the basic features of PL are as follows:

1. Trainee works at his own pace.
2. Through a series of logical steps.
3. All leading to pre-defined goals or objectives.
4. By actively responding.
5. And by mastering each step.
6. He receives feedback information (or knowledge of results).
7. Which motivates him to continue.
8. The programme is thoroughly tested before it is printed.

9. SYNDICATE METHOD

Syndicate method is one of the methods of training. When the number is large, they are called as group and when the number is small, they are called as syndicate. There are minor differences between group discussion and syndicate method. But the method of working is the same for both groups.

Definition

According to ILO: Any method of working, which a small group may use to achieve a particular purpose, might fairly be described as a syndicate method. The essence of the syndicate method is that man should learn from each other and contribute their own experience to the fullest. The main work of the tutorial staff is to organize the work so that this mixture of experience takes place to the maximum extent possible within the duration of the course.

The syndicate method is designed to provide the participant an environment that would help him:

(*a*) to reflect critically on his own work and experience;

(*b*) to update his knowledge of new concepts and techniques with the help of other participants;

(*c*) to develop sound judgment through greater insight into human behaviour.

Advantages of this method

1. It secures high level of involvement from the participants. There is friendliness as well as healthy competition within each syndicate so also among syndicates.
2. For the practicing managers their own experience is the starting point of the syndicate method. Through various work assignments, the participants can assimilate new concepts, techniques, and information more easily. Thus, it is a process of self-education and development for participants.
3. The availability of the directing staff and outside experts can stimulate critical thinking on the part of the participants and enable them to bring out the best.
4. It also gives the participant a practice of communicating with his colleagues. It provides an environment different from his daily work situation.
5. Working in syndicates involves interaction over an extended period of time and living together with a cross-section of the people from different types of organizations. This results in a broad minded approach to managerial problems.

Mechanics of the Method

1. The participants are divided into groups consisting of ten. These groups are called as syndicates.

2. Each syndicate functions as a team. It has representatives from cross-section of organizations and on the other hand it is a balanced management team with man from functional areas of management.
3. The syndicates are given assignments, which have to be finished and a report submitted in a specified time.
4. By rotation, each member of the syndicate becomes the leader for completing a specific task.
5. Each assignment to a syndicate is given in the form of brief. This is carefully prepared document by the trainer.
6. Each syndicate is placed under a number of the directing staff who acts as a resource person rather than as a trainer. He gives them advice and guidance without giving his own answers for tasks assigned.
7. Each syndicate is required to submit a report, which is circulated to other syndicates for evaluation.
8. The leader of each syndicate is required to present the view of his team at a joint session of all groups.

How to prepare to lead a discussion

1. Determine the overall objectives
2. Define the topics clearly.
3. Consider the group.
4. Prepare a detailed discussion outline.
5. Have everything ready (materials, handouts, equipment, etc).

How to lead a discussion

1. *Get off to a good start*
   - Start the meeting on time.
   - Try to make the group feel at ease.
2. *Lead into the discussion*
   - State the general purpose of the discussion.
   - Announce the topic clearly.

- Explain the discussion procedures.
- Introduce the topic.

3. *Guide the discussion*
   - Encourage the participation by all.
   - Control the over talkative member.
   - Draw out the shy member.
   - Avoid personal arguments.
   - Keep the discussion on the subject.
   - Summarize frequently.
   - Use audio-visual aids.
4. *Summarize the discussion*
   - Review the highlights of the discussion.
   - Review the conclusions reached.
   - Make clear what has been discussed.
   - End on a high note.

Questions and their uses in discussion leading

1. *Uses of questions*
   - To get all members of the group involved in discussion.
   - To awaken interest.
   - To find out what previous knowledge on the subject the members have.
   - To keep the discussion moving.
   - To stop private conversation.
   - To prevent monopolization by one member.
   - To highlight the important aspects of the subject.
   - To check on the groups assimilation on the subject matter.
2. *Types of questions*

   There are two types of questions:

   (a) General questions; and

   (b) Direct questions

3. *General rules on the use of questions*
    - Questions should be brief, clear and simple.
    - Direct question should be distributed at random.
    - Question should cover one point only.
    - Question should be related to the ability and experience of the person.
    - Give the members of the group time to think before answering.
    - Don't use leading questions.

10. SELF-MANAGED LEARNING

Self-managed learning is a technique of training through which an individual is learning himself without others help. The trainee takes the responsibility for decisions about:

- what to learn
- how to learn
- when to learn
- where to learn
- why to learn

Managing their own learning means that the person is using wide range of opportunities for learning. These include:

- learning from others around them
- travel
- reading
- projects
- being coached/mentored

Self-Managed Learning Principles

There are seven Ss', for the learning principles, which are discussed below:

1. *Strategic*

SML demands that people take a strategic stance in relation to their own learning. Strategy here means thinking long-term and with the big picture in mind. People may need to get a sense of their current abilities, qualities, values and interests to prepare for future career and life opportunities. Often it needs a context in which the person can clarify this for them to become more strategic.

2. *Syllabus-free*

There is no required curriculum or syllabus in SML, the learning is driven by the real needs of individuals and their organization. Learners may need assistance to help them to make their choices of what to learn.

3. *Self-managed*

Self-managing includes the necessary interaction with others. People have to take responsibility for their own learning.

4. *Shared*

SML requires learners to connect with others and especially to integrate their learning with organizational needs. A learning contract is more than just a fancy name for a personal development plan or an action plan. A learning contract is different because:

- It is a seriously written document that is negotiated between the individual and relevant interested parties.
- It is a living document that individuals refer to regularly.

5. *Supported*

Learners are supported in meeting the goals they set themselves in their learning contract. One support structure is the learning set. The set is the primary place where each person negotiates their learning contract and reports progress on it. The set meets every four to six weeks and provides a place for both support and challenge. Participants comment that the set provides a unique, cost-effective forum to push individuals to learn in depth and to solve real business problems.

6. *Structured*

SML provides a structure in order to help learning. The learners decide for themselves how to use the structure. SML programmes need to be carefully designed to suit the organization, its culture and its direction.

7. *Stretching*

SML is not an easy option. The requirement to set goals and meet them is a tough-minded approach to learning. To meet regularly with colleagues to discuss progress means that learners have to keep to their agreed plans or change them.

11. OPEN LEARNING

Open learning (OL) has close relationship to self-managed learning. SML can be combined with open learning. Open learning is one where the student is not restricted in any of the ways that he or she undertakes learning. The media used can be any thing, the location can be any where, the choice of subject can be any thing and the learning pace is entirely left to the student.

OL in a company normally centers around an OL center which is frequently renamed as the Flexible Learning Center, the Personal Learning Center and Learning Resource Center. Basically, all these centers are the same—a collection of various media, equipment to run them and personnel to support the students or users. Some companies spend a fortune on making their centers both pleasant and functional to use.

Limitations of OL

1. It is costly in terms of trainer, travel and other associated cost and also in the cost of the trainee being away from his workplace.
2. The course, once finished can not be revisited except by reference to course note or doing it all again.
3. The quality of the course is partly dependent on the performance of the trainer.
4. The trainer has to contend with trainees who are joining the course at different knowledge levels.

12. ON-THE-JOB TRAINING

The trainee is taught in the physical environment in which he eventually will be required to perform his task.

Advantages

(i) The problem of transfer of learning is virtually eliminated.

(ii) On-the-job training allows him to practice precisely what he is expected to do after the completion of his training.

(iii) Trainee becomes acclimated to the daily operating procedures.

(iv) Trainee provided with the opportunity to associate with the same peers, superiors and subordinates he will work with after training.

(v) Offers the opportunity for maximum control and the unilization of the relevant reinforcements, because the reinforcements are usually the same during learning and subsequent.

Disadvantages

(i) On-the-job training is inappropriate if the material to be taught is rational, logical and intellectual.

(ii) Fails to get away the trainee from the job and its pressures, and presents him from working in a climate in which "party-line" thinking is encouraged.

1. *How to plan On-The-Job Training*

(a) Determine what you want the participants to learn.

(b) Break materials to be taught into operations and arrange them in order of priorities.

(c) Identify background requirements.

(d) Consider the group-estimate what they are likely to know, feel, think about their jobs already.

(e) Assess training material requirements and check their availability.

(f) Assign time and place for the operations to be learnt.

2. *How to Instruct On-The-Job*

(a) *Prepare the worker*

(i) Put him at ease — act natural, be friendly

(ii) Find out what he already knows about the job and stimulate his interest in it.

(iii) Develop the importance of the job which is to be taught.

(b) *Present the Operation*

(i) Tell - Tell him want the job entails

– Telling helps trainee remember things he sees.

(ii) Show and explain, telling or showing is not sufficient.

– Draw his attention to the heights and explain slowly while showing.

– Have him ask questions as you go along in your demonstration.

(c) *Performance Try-out*

(i) Encourage the learner to do the job which has been presented.

(ii) Provide the learner with the necessary materials and equipment to do the job.

(iii) Observe the learner carefully as he does the job

(iv) Ask the learner questions

(v) Permit the learner to continue with the job - but check.

And reteach whenever errors in procedure or understanding are observed.

(d) *Follow-up*

(i) Put him on his own

(*ii*) Tell him where to go if he needs help

(*iii*) Observe his performance regularly and correct mistakes promptly and tactfully.

(*iv*) *Questioning:* By asking questions draw out facts which are essential in teaching the job.

- Questioning keeps the learner's mind active and concentrated on what is being taught.
- Heightens learner's interest
- Stimulates his confidence by affording him an opportunity to show his knowledge.
- Compels learner to think through and does not permit him to remain passive.
- Enables instructor to know if the learner is actually following him.

(*e*) *Combination Methods*

The instructor should not rely on any one of the three/ four methods outlined, but should use all of them in combination, according to the nature of the job or knowledge being taught. For example:

1. Tell and Show
2. Show and Question
3. Illustrate all Tell

Steps in On-the-Job Training

The following steps are recommended to make the on-the-job training successful.

1. *Prepare the leaner*

(*a*) Put the learner at ease — Relieve the tension.

(*b*) Explain why he is being taught.

(*c*) Create interest, encourage questions, find out what the learner already knows about this job.

(*d*) Explain the whole job and relate it to some job the trainee already knows.

(e) Place the trainee as close to the normal working position as possible.
(f) Familiarize the trainee with equipment, materials, tools, etc.

2. *Present the operation*
(a) Explain quantity and quality requirements.
(b) Go through the job at the normal work pace.
(c) Go through the job at a slow pace several times.
(d) Again go through the job at a slow pace, several pace and explain the key points.

3. *Do a try out*
(a) While going through the job, correct the mistakes, do some of the complicated steps for few minutes.
(b) Run the job at the normal pace.
(c) Gradually build up the skill and speed.

4. *Follow-up*
(a) Designate to whom the trainee should go for help.
(b) Gradually decrease supervision against quality and quantity standards.
(c) Correct faulty work patterns before they become a habit.
(d) Encourage the good work.

13. MENTORING

The origins of mentoring lie in Greek mythology, where Mentor acted as an adviser, counselor, to the young prince Telemachus. Mentoring has evolved through apprenticeship to become a widely applicable means of transferring wisdom in almost any area of endeavor. The European Mentoring Center defines it 'off-line help by one person to another in making significant transitions in knowledge, work or thinking'.

Off-line: Because the mentor normally has to be outside the chain of command or discipline, in order to establish a relationship of openness and trust.

Help: Because the mentor responds to a variety of needs, both emotional and intellectual, hands-on and hands-off.

By one person to another: Because, although the mentor would typically be older and more senior than the mentee, this is not always so. What counts is the depth and breadth of relevant, transferable experience.

Significant transitions: Because without some clear developmental purpose, the relationship is unlikely to deliver meaningful results.

Knowledge, work or thinking: Because the transition may be in any of these areas.

Responsibilities of the Core Roles

Mentor plays four different roles as follows:

Coach

- Help mentee set viable personal goals.
- Explain why you think something needs to be challenged.
- Probe with questions to challenge thinking.
- Help mentee accept and think through challenge.
- Offer help in dealing with it.

Guardian

- Assess barriers and ways around them.
- Open doors.
- Know your strengths and weaknesses as a role model.
- Understand and explain the politics behind operational problems.

Networker

Understand what a mentee needs networking for:

- Getting things done.
- Expand their knowledge.
- Recognize who and what you/your mentee know.

- Gather the information to make the best recommendation.
- Discuss the best approach.

Counsellor

- Actively listen and make sure you understand their side.
- Keep it upbeat by refocusing on positive outcomes.
- Use your experience to help the mentee to come to own conclusions.
- Explain and justify your comments.

Why the sudden popularity of mentoring?

1. Increased disillusionment with classroom training as the primary means of learning in organizations.
2. The rapid speed of investors in people has focused attention on one-to-one methods of employee development.
3. Recognition that appraisals often do not lead to any real changes in the competence of the appraisee.
4. Increasing emphasis on self-development.
5. Increasing complexity of career paths.
6. New organization structures.
7. Some organizations have gone even further in recreating their structures.

What makes an effective mentoring scheme?

1. Begin with a clear rationale and purpose.
2. Understand the development climate within the organization.
3. Establish a formal structure to administer the scheme.
4. Select and match mentors and mentees carefully. Key principles for selection include:
   - balancing ability to establish rapport against potential:
   - allowing the mentee at least some opportunity to select from a pool of trained mentors.

- making all relationships probationary for the first few meetings and building in an automatic review.

5. Provide training for both mentors and mentees.
6. The purpose of the helping relationship has to be clear.
7. Measurement and review are important to identify problems with the scheme and with individual relationships, and to demonstrate that the scheme is delivering results.

Skills of Mentoring

1. Good communication skills, especially listening and questioning.
2. A sense of humour.
3. Good rapport building.
4. An interest in developing others.
5. An interest in continuing to develop themselves.

14. COUNSELING

Counseling is a professional activity, which can be done only by a person wishing to be a counselor and who can meet the conditions of confidentiality, independence, and impartiality. Counseling is a vocational activity with a specific role.

Skills Needed for Counseling

1. *Listening:* The counselor should be a great listener to understand the problems of the people.
2. *Attending:* He should be attentive to the task and focuses on things like attitude, mindset, and rapport.
3. *Self awareness:* The trainer should aware in terms of thoughts, emotions, and behaviours.
4. *Verbal interventions:* This overlaps with listening. The verbal interventions on questioning, scene setting, challenging, and self-disclosure.
5. *Empathy:* This is getting close to experiencing what the other person is feeling is essential.

6. *Problem-solving:* Techniques which help people solve problems. This is a practical aspect of using counseling skills.
7. *Confidentiality:* This is a core condition for the ethical use of counseling skills.

Situations where Counseling can be used

1. *Crisis and copping:* Under this situation personal or home-related problems, which affect the person at work are discussed (marriage difficulties, debt, drinking, etc). Work related problems like stress, strain, etc can also be counseled.
2. *Fitness and function:* Personal improvements enabling us to be fit in some way, e.g., confidence, peace of mind, motivation, etc. There are many organizational roles, which would benefit from these skills in a fitness and function context-roles such as supervisor, manager, trainer, etc. All these have the need to function better and to keep others function better.

15. BEHAVIOUR MODELING

This is a method of training in which trainees are shown how a task should be performed and then practice the task with feedback. This is based on the idea that workers learn best when they see how a task should be performed and then practice the task with feedback. This method is similar to role-play in that trainees act out situations playing certain roles.

Steps in Behaviour Modeling

1. *Present an overview of the material:* This usually consists of a brief lecture that describes the objectives of training and the importance of the skill to be learned.
2. *Describe the procedural steps:* The trainees learn the one best way to handle a situation. Case and role play methods on the other hand stress the variety of ways to handle a situation and do not emphasise any one particular approach.

3. *Model or Demonstrate the procedural steps:* The trainee is shown a model of how the task is to be performed correctly. This model is usually presented in the form of a video tape or live demonstration.
4. *Allow guided practice:* The trainees then practice the modeled behaviours. This procedure forces the trainees to correct mistakes as soon as they are made, assuring them an opportunity to practice the correct way of performing a task.

16. ON-SITE OBSERVATION

This involves touring of organizational establishments, observing of related individual jobs, and meeting of authorities on job-oriented activities.

Purpose

The idea is to familiarize participants with various job-oriented activities in organizational establishments whose concepts and principles have been discussed in class and possibly learnt on the job.

Procedure

Such trainings are conducted individually or collectively with the purpose of observing individual job and functions and their relationship to each other and how they contribute to the departmental and/or total corporate objectives.

Advantages

(*a*) Provides the opportunity to observe operations in totality.
(*b*) Reinforces what has been learnt in class or the job.
(*c*) Clearly show the relationship of job to each other.
(*d*) Introduces the trainee to possible problem areas.
(*e*) Gives the trainee hints on improvement possibilities.

Disadvantages

(*a*) It can sometimes be boring because every incumbent is desirous of talking much about his job.
(*b*) The trainee is given more to learn than he can reasonably absorb.
(*c*) Details are hidden.

17. FILMS AND VIDEOS AS TRAINING TECHNIQUES

Films

In the era of science and media explosion, films play a crucial role as a tool of training technique. Closely associated with films are the videos. Videos are of recent origin and films are as old as a century. Professional media organizations regularly prepare films on various aspects of training. Some of the case studies on organizations are also developed by films. The case histories of successful managers as well as successful entrepreneurs are made as films and are available for ready use.

Preparation

The film presenter (Trainer) should do certain preparatory work.

1. View the film completely.
2. Make note on the following:
   (a) Significant scenes which relate to his training message and his organisation.
   (b) Significant phrases and expressions used by the characters which typify employees in his organization.
   (c) Any training points picked out or captioned in the film.
   (d) Any 'below the line training points in the film. These will be points not captioned or mentioned in the dialogue but dropped in for the sharp-eyed trainer to notice.
3. Read the guide as to how to use the film.
4. See the film again.

Quality of Films

Films are prepared like any other cinema films or documentary films. The production process involves the script writing, choosing the role players, location, background, editing, directing, etc. While preparing a film the main consideration is quality.

Quality covers two main areas — production and content. Quality of production — script writing, direction, acting — is vital in a television age, where so much knowledge and information is communicated in an entertaining way through a little box in the corner of the room. The viewing public has become extremely critical.

A film or video programme which is of an inferior production standard to broadcast television immediately produces a credibility gap, no matter how worthy or job-related the contents of the programme. Today a number of training film production companies use top-class directors, writers and actors to ensure high production and entertainment values in all their training programmes.

Quality of content depends on two things — the first is that the film writer/producer has researched and distilled the myriad training points which could be included in, say, a film on how to sell or how to run a meeting into a sensible and memorable shortlist of key training points, and has found a way of communicating these points both clearly and accurately in training terms. The second ingredient is that the content is right for his audience and for his organization. In other words is the style of the film acceptable?

Trainers should think twice about a film which highlights or captions twenty or so discrete training points in fifteen minutes. Audience retention of these points will be low.

Part of the trainer's decision will be governed by the style of the film and the place it will occupy in the training session. For instance, some trainers like to use films as curtain raisers, some as a discussion tool, others as a means of building role-plays by extending some cameo scenes in the film, and some people prefer to use film as a summary of a particular training session.

Using the Film

The trainer is now in a position to decide when and how to use the film in his programme.

In the main the training films available can be divided into two types — Case study films and wrong way/right way films.

Case Study Films

Case studies often show a series of problems or mistakes.

A trainer using these programmes is well advised to use such a film as a curtain raiser. A case study film covering, say, the role of supervisor, can be used at the beginning of a one- or two-day training programme, to promote a general discussion. (Or, of course, it can be applied at the beginning of a shorter training session.) The advantage of using a case study film at the beginning of a long training programme is that the film then gives a framework to the rest of thc teaching. 'Case studies' also save delegates from having to quote potentially embarrassing or divisive real instances. They can talk about the people in the film, instead of colleagues and superiors. A case study applied in this way gives both the delegates and the trainer a common form of reference. Individual scenes within the case study highlighting particular aspects of, say, a supervisor's role, for instance handling discipline problems or how to train on the job, can then be used at a later stage as 'clips', and more detailed discussion can then take place on these subjects.

Wrong Way/Right Way Films

There are many films on the market which take a specific subject and divide this subject into discrete sections. An individual scene is used to demonstrate the wrong way of handling each aspect, followed by a right way scene. Occasionally an analogy is used to demonstrate the 'right way' or to build a natural bridge to the correct way of approaching the subject.

Some trainers show films from start to finish without stopping. A more imaginative use of this type of film is to stop the film after each 'wrong way' scene. This gives the trainer the opportunity of working with the group in one/all of the following ways:

1. To hold a discussion on what went wrong in the scene.
2. To hold a discussion on how the situation should have been approached.
3. To ask people to take over the characters portrayed in the 'wrong way' scene and to get themselves out of the difficulties — in other words role-play themselves out of the situation.
4. To take the 'right way' points produced ask the delegates to put their view into action, in other words role-play their suggested solution.

Having made delegates work on and think about a certain part of the film, the trainer can then move on to show the 'right way' scene in the film and compare this way with the delegates' suggested methods of dealing with the subject.

In certain instances the 'right way' scenes depicted in the film can still be improved upon. The trainer can use these scenes to promote further discussion with delegates, to ask them what they felt about the suggested solution and whether it could have been improved. At the end of a session of this type the film should be shown in its entirety.

Now a days specialized TV channels broadcast number of films relating to training programmes. Such programmes are available through network.

Videos

Compared to films, videos are convenient and they can be displayed anywhere with a computer. Preparations needed to display a video are very simple and the time taken will also be very short.

The vitality of video sparked new creative approaches which avoided the somewhat set-piece approach of many training films.

In offices, the videocassette player and TV sets were far more acceptable than the more formal procedures associated with a film presentation.

Video brought immediacy, accessibility, informality and lower costs. It also brought a vastly larger market for the producers and greatly increased the use of the medium by the organizations who were their customers.

Currently, video is used for in-house training by many organizations, a number of which produce their own programmes. Some companies have permanently transferred their allegiance from film to video, and are producing or commissioning sophisticated training programmes in a multi-media format, with video as a central component.

The TV set and the VCR have become part of the training structure used to a greater or lesser extent by most organizations with a training requirement.

A video training programme can capture the distillation of the knowledge and expertise possessed by the authors. The training content can be definitively organized within the programme and its subsequent use imposes a degree of consistency difficult to achieve in other ways.

Video has become an accepted tool of the trainer. It extends his contribution to meeting the training requirement, relieves him of some of the routine teaching burden, and increases the overall efficiency and acceptability of training within the organization.

The objective of distance learning is to transfer a high percentage of the teaching burden from the central training establishment of the trainer's locale. Traditionally, the scarce resource represented by the teacher if made available economically through the mechanism of a number of trainees attending a class or course. Where there is no alternative, this process is unquestioned and its inherent inefficiencies and rigidities are unchallenged.

The objective of distance learning is to revolutionise this process by taking training to the trainee. The theoretical benefits are obvious: the trainee no longer has to conform to a timetable or attend a course at a set time or place. The unproductive expense on travel, accommodation and subsistence is eliminated. A distance learning system can provide flexibility and more efficient use of the training budget.

There is, of course, nothing new in the concept of distance learning. Reference has been made to the self-teach programmes used by many large organizations. All correspondence courses are a form of distance learning, and programmed learning techniques have been applied through self-teaching programmes using both audio-visual and print media.

Video has a major contribution to make as an element in a distance learning progrmme. It is inherently stimulating people remember more of what they see — and it secures the undivided attention of the viewer. However, it suffers from the defects listed earlier: it is passive; it is not adaptable; and it lacks the ability to monitor the trainee's performance.

18. PROJECT-BASED TRAINING

Meaning

This is one of the latest training techniques introduced in the corporate sector. In addition to inculcating the training skills to the trainees, an exposure is given to the trainees by means of giving exercises in the form of project preparation. Projects may be in the form of assessment, feasibilities, business plans, etc.

The project is selected on the basis of its suitability to meet the individual needs of the trainees, but must be a viable commercial project that is required by the company, e.g. a study into the viability of word processing for the company: or a report on the competitors promotion techniques within a specific market sector.

Artificial or theoretical project will not allow the training objectives to be effectively met, as trainees and tutors will see it only as a training exercise — to work effectively. They must have the pressure of a commercial evaluation on completion of the project, for which they will be held responsible.

The size, complexity and length of the project are not critical, except to ensure that it will expose the trainees to the necessary area of skill development for sufficient time to give them the opportunity to achieve the training objectives. This technique involves three distinct roles: the trainee, the tutor and the trainer, defined as follows:

Trainee(s)

One or more people with clearly defined training needs selected by their managers as priority areas for skill development, which may be achieved by working under guidance on a specific project.

Tutor(s)

One or more people with the knowledge and skill to guide the trainee(s) working on the project, in one or more of the specific area identified for skill development.

Trainer

A neutral guide and mentor with no involvement in the project, but who has strong counselling and analytical skills.

The principle of the technique is that the trainee(s) and tutor(s) work together on the project, fulfilling different roles. The role of the trainee(s) is to carry out particular tasks within the project and to contribute to the conclusions and final presentation. The role of the tutor(s) is to guide the trainee(s) in specific tasks within the project, to be available for consultation on any aspect and to guide the group in reaching conclusions for final presentation.

The trainer's role is to oversee the training aspect of the project with control over trainees and tutors. It does not include responsibility for the achievement of project results: this role falls to the project leader, who may be one of the trainees, one of the tutors, or in larger projects a third party with specific related skills.

Why is project —based training needed?

Through the 1960s and early 1970s training progressed in every aspect. A range of new methods developed to meet virtually every need, with sopesticated aids that could put the trainee into almost any situation.

In smaller companies, where common training needs rarely exist for more than two or three people at the same time, this need for a more selective training method has always existed. Now these companies are seeking more urgently to develop skills many new areas.

These demands have resulted in a proliferation of specialist courses' with companies using a far wider range of outside programmes ranging from one-, two- or three-day seminars to the day, week or block release concept.

This attempt to satisfy individual needs through outside courses has only be a part of the answer. The line manager still has to achieve job-related skill development where the course does exist, and in many cases relevant courses cannot be found.

In these cases, where specific individual knowledge and skill development is needed, particularly when it is related to specific company activities, the use of project-based training techniques can be the most cost effective method.

Merits of Project-based Training

It is a method of training designed to develop the knowledge and skills of an individual or group of trainees, in the course of working on a genuine project.

It can be used as a technique on its own, with the project designed to expose the trainee to a practical situation within which learning can take place; for example, the use of the research project into a new market to develop a salesman. As knowledge of that market whilst at the same time developing his skills in market research.

It can be used within an off-the-job training environment, where a project is built into a training course to allow skill development, such as allowing a group of new trainee salesmen to make their own video training programmes on selling technique as part of their training.

And it can be used as part of a planned development programme which involves a trainee in a number of formal training courses, with a project linking the courses to give the opportunity to put into practice the new areas of knowledge and skill.

Perhaps the most complex use of the project-based training technique is when the method is used in-company to develop the knowledge and skills of a group of people, where training needs differ, but a project can be used to link each requirement.

When should project-based training be used?

Project-based training should be considered when:

1. One or more staff have specific training needs, particularly in skill development area when;
   - The needs cannot easily be met by on-the-job training or by attending specific training courses, for example, the need to train three or four people in controlling a new product launch.
   - The needs of each person are different.
   - The needs are similar but the degree of training need differs.
   - The needs are related to the application of knowledge to a specific task, such as one person actually controlling a product launch.
2. Training is needed in areas directly related to the company's own business — a particular need in the sales operation is for a wider range of functions, e.g. sales analysis, customer records, area forecasting.
3. The knowledge and skill exists within the company but the running of an in-house training course is not practical because:
   - Skill development is the prime objective.
   - Those with the knowledge and skills are not good trainers.

- The group with the training needs is too small to justify a training course

4. These with the training needs have a negative attitude towards training but will accept involvement in a company project: perhaps problem with older, more senior or more experienced staff who feels training is beneath them.
5. One or more people have training needs that could be met through work on a project, and separately one or more people have training needs which are linked to skill development in on-the job training, counselling or group interaction. In these cases the use of project-based training can be justified separately by alternative methods.
6. The need is to develop the skills of a group of people in a new working environment where the secondary objective is to achieve a closer working relationship between those in the group — a situation faced by many companies, again especially with the expansion of the Computer
7. The training needs relate to a specialist subject about which the company training staff know too little to conduct direct training — especially important in the areas of computers, accounts, specialist products, production or engineering subjects when related to marketing and sales.
8. Skills being introduced to the company by a consultant or adviser will be needed by a number of people within the company. In this case the consultant/adviser may take the role of project leader or, if qualified, the role of trainer.

Role of the Trainer

To succeed, a project-based training scheme must be controlled by a competent person taking the neutral role of a trainer. To fulfill this role the person must have the skills to:

- analyse training needs;
- counsel managers, tutor and trainees;

- act as a neutral observer within the project team;
- conduct on-the-job training related to the role of the tutor;
- control any inter-reactions within the group through the tutors;
- monitor and guide the progress of the group in achieving the training objectives.

It is not necessary for the trainer to have a detailed knowledge of the project area, although an understanding of the subjects is necessary to ensure the monitoring of training progress is accurate.

In some companies the use of an outside specialist in the trainer's role will give the necessary skill and neutrality. At all times the trainer must remain in a neutral role within the project—the role is one of trainer, not a member of the project team.

An Extended Training Plan

The project technique is of particular value when used as part of the planned development of an individual over a period of months, such as the development of a good field sales trainer in readiness for movement into line management, or the development of a good line manager to become involved in more senior management.

In such cases the overall training objectives and plans must be analysed to identify: the areas of knowledge and skill development that can/will be developed through formal training; and the priority areas where development of this knowledge and skill must be related to the Company. A project is then selected with management and this is built into the over all development programme. A tutor must be identified, (the trainer, the trainer's line manager or another manager) to be available throughout the project.

The development programme can then be operated with the project giving the opportunity for skill development within the company's own environment.

Benefits of Project-based Training

To summarise if the training project has been properly set up, tightly controlled during its operation, and carefully monitored at all times by the trainer, the conclusion should be that the individual or group of trainees, each with specific training needs, will have gained considerable learning by partial experience, through involvement in a constructive commercial project.

Effective skill development in a practical working situation will have been achieved.

The technique, whether used in the complex in-house group situation, in the extended individual development programme. As part of skill development within a training course will give a practical and valuable proven training aid that is both flexible for the trainer and enjoyable for those being trained

The case study that follows highlights a number of the points made and shows some elements of the principles discussed at work in practice.

19. COMPETENCY-BASED TRAINING

When organizations compete with each other to capture markets and to bring more customers under their fold, the quality of products and services must be improved and updated. When technology is changed in production process and service sectors, to meet the demands of the new situations organizations must go for training programmes based on industry-specific standards.

The term competency-based training, is meant to mean something like an educational process that is based on specific competencies that have been previously identified.

Competency-based training (CBT) is a way of globally approaching vocational training that has its main focus on what the person can actually do in the workplace as a result of the training. It is concerned with training to industry-specific standards rather than with the individual's achievement in comparison to others in the group.

When we look at a traditional time-based approach to education, we can easily see that if the programme has been correctly designed initially, it will meet the same criteria. By 'traditional time-based education' mean a properly structured training programme with clearly defined objectives that are measurable. If they are measurable, we can say that the trainee can or cannot do what they were supported to be able to do at the conclusion of the training.

Recognition of prior learning

Recognition of prior learning (RPL) forms only a small part of CBT. 'Recognition of prior learning' is acknowledging the fact that sometimes (most times?) our trainees already know some of what the instruction is about and therefore allowing them credit for what they have previously learnt. Applying this to its full extent, a person can be awarded certification without ever attending training. One needs to be aware also that recognition of participants' previous knowledge and skills can also be considered with traditional training programmes.

Difference between CBT and Ordinary Training

The traditional time-based approach to education initially identifies a training or learning need and sets about to fill that need. When the focus is on CBT, it may appear that the designer identifies only the more easily measurable competencies.

A CBT system is made up of two components. First, there is an instrument aimed at a learner-achieving competency in precisely defined skills, and knowledge to specified standards, under specific conditions. Second, there should be certification based on the correct assessment of competencies achieved both at on-the-job and off-the-job.

These competencies should be agreed to by all parties involved, that is, training authorities, employee groups, industry groups, trade groups, relevant councils, employee representative groups, employees etc. This will allow for more mobility of competencies, both in industry and location.

Steps in Developing a CBT Programme

There are five major steps in the development of a CBT programme:

1. An extensive consultative process between relevant parties or groups identifies the relevant skills needed for a particular position in a particular industry.
2. The skills that are identified are organised into appropratiate groups from which learning can be developed.
3. The physical materials that the programme will be based on, are developed. Sometimes these will be more extensive than those in traditional-type training programmes.
4. The people administering the CBT will need to be trained. Their instructional style may need to be modified to allow for more flexibility (but not flexibility of outcomes). These trainers will also need to become aware of the assessment criteria, which must be consistent.
5. Ways of recording information are identified and established. Generally the administrative component of CBT requires far more effort than that required for traditional training programmes.

Competency Standards

Competency standards provide the specification of the knowledge and skill, and the application of that knowledge and skill to the standard of performance required in employment. There are three interrelated types of standards:

1. *Industry standards*

   The national competency standards endorsed for a specific industry.
2. *Cross-industry standards*

   Based on competencies common to a range of industries. These are generally used to facilitate portability, consistency and efficiency in the development of standards.

3. *Enterprise standards*

   Standards which consist of competencies developed and/or used specifically at enterprise level. They may or may not include industry or cross-industry standards.

   A competency standard has the following format:

- *Elements of competency:* Describe actions or outcomes that are demonstrable or assessable. They are written in 'input' and 'output' terms, and, in relation to units of competency, they are the lowest logical and identifiable sub groupings of actions and knowledge which contribute to and build a unit.
- *Performance criteria:* These are statements that an assessor can use to judge the performance specified in the elements of competence to a level acceptable in employment. The performance criteria must be written to provide a link between the competency and its evidence of achievement.
- *Range-of-variables statement:* This specifies the range of contexts and conditions to which the performance criteria apply.
- *Evidence guide:* The evidence guide is an optimal part of the standard, covering contexts for assessment, critical aspects of a unit and its relationship to other units, and the required evidence of competency.

Conclusion

CBT identifies specific outcomes through the involvement of all relevant parties. It improves the mobility of knowledge and skills for the learner. CBT sometimes creates extravagant system or number of systems that are expensive in their design, structure and administration. Education needs to more clearly target its resources on the educational process, rather than creating more bureaucracy.

Many experts state that it is an expensive system to design structure and administer. They also believe that there may be an additional expense because sometimes the programme is out of date before it is even released! This is due to the amount of time required to set these programmes up.

Summary

• In this chapter various training techniques and methods are discussed. They are: lecture method, case study, business games, role-play, in-basket training, experimental learning, IT related, programmed training, syndicate method, self-managed learning, open learning, on-the-job-training, mentoring, on-site observation, films and videos as training methods, project based and competency-based training.

Self-Learning Activity

Try to answer the following questions on your own:

1. Discuss about syndicate method.
2. What is behaviour modeling?
3. Write notes on: *(a)* Project-based training; *(b)* competency based training.

16

Trainer and his Role in Training

Quality of Training

The following factors decide the quality of training.

1. *Commitment to the goal of the organization:* Individual employee as well as the organization must commit themselves to the goals of the organization, by way of making training as an important input and investment.
2. *Training environment:* The training environment must be conducive to the trainees. As far as possible the venue of training should be away from the work place.
3. *Professionalization of the trainers:* The trainers must be well qualified and must have enough experience to handle the experienced trainees.
4. *Funds and resources:* Adequate funds must be allotted for training by the organization. Supplementary resources needed for training must also be allotted.
5. *Duration of training:* When training is opted for short duration, a better quality can be given than training which takes long duration.
6. *Number of trainees:* Lesser the number of trainees higher will be the quality of training.
7. *Knowledge required:* If the training requires the teaching of multiplicity of knowledge, naturally the quality may go down. So it is better to teach limited number of areas.

8. *Background of trainees:* If the trainees have adequate experience and educational background the quality of training can be very high. When they are exposed to more training, the quality of training will also be high.
9. *Place of training:* If the location of the training has a conducive climate, away from the city noises and pollution, the quality of the training may be high.

Training to Trainers (TOT)

Why training is needed for the trainers?

1. *Learning/training is a continuous process:* When an individual enters into teaching and training profession, learning has become a continuous process. There cannot be any gap and any gap may lead to knowledge deficiency.
2. *To keep abreast to latest knowledge:* As knowledge is expanding day after day, it is inevitable for the trainers to keep themselves abreast with the latest knowledge. Such knowledge can be taught to them by various methods of teaching, referring library and contacting experts.
3. *To know the latest training techniques:* Training techniques in the field of management and related areas are changing very often. With increase in knowledge of subjects and increase in individual potentialities, training techniques must also be changed. Example, change in techniques after the introduction of computers.
4. *To teach the trainees effectively:* A good teacher alone can deliver good teaching to students. When a trainer undergoes effective training by means of learning new knowledge and latest techniques of teaching, he can import the same to his students effectively.

Preparations needed for the trainer

1. *Thorough understanding of the subject:* Before a trainer launches his training activities, he must be thorough with the subject, which he is going to teach. Good amount of referring of library and journals are prerequisites for understanding the subjects.

2. *Ability to communicate:* A trainer must be able to communicate very freely with his trainees. His teaching must be easily understandable to the trainees. He must take care of his personality, posture, facial expression, movement, gesticulation, eye contact, etc. He must also be ready for question-answer sessions and discussion and debate with the trainees.
3. *Setting the learning climate:* While going to the class the trainer must have a free and open mind. He should have a smiling face and should express a charming pose to the trainees. He must treat the trainees as equals and must give respect to their views. Mutual respect and sharing of the common goals should be taken care of. He must provide a climate of desire to learn by the trainees.
4. *Applying the learning methods:* The trainer must prepare various methods of learning to the trainees. The application of teaching methods may vary from group of trainees. He must also be familiar with using of audio-visual aids, computer CDs, etc.
5. *Right personality and motivation to train:* The trainer should have well equipped physical personality to impress the trainees. Dress, mannerism, movement, willingness to listen, to have an open mind and motivation to train or certain qualities required of the trainers.

Role of the Trainer in Training

1. *Understand the training needs of the target group:* The trainer must have prior knowledge about the training needs of future trainees. Then only he can prepare himself to reach the levels of the trainees.
2. *Set the learning climate:* The trainer must create a learning climate during every session by means of creating a free class atmosphere. He must also give freedom to the trainees in terms of his access to questions.
3. *Explain the contents of the training programme at the beginning even before the programme begins:* The trainer must prepare various aspects of training and give the materials or

handouts to the trainees. The handouts must contain details relating to the daily routines and individual trainers curriculum.

4. *Respect the trainees' views:* A trainer should not treat the trainees inferior to him. Many of the trainees might have acquired more theoretical and practical knowledge. Such views must be respected by the trainer.
5. *Prepare thoroughly:* As noted earlier, a trainer must go to the class having prepared thoroughly. He must be in a position to answer the questions raised by the trainees with exact facts and figures.
6. *Prepare teaching aids:* The relevant teaching aids must be prepared quite earlier by the trainer. As far as possible a trainer must use audio-visual equipments, OHPs, etc.
7. *Encourage learners' feedback:* Every trainer must get feedback from the trainees about the training programme, the contents, the impression about his teaching and the effectiveness of the whole programme. Such feedback will be useful for the total evaluation of the training programme.
8. *Keep punctuality:* A trainer must be an example to the trainees in keeping punctuality by way of attending class in time, confining his lecture to the subject and completing the course programme in time and as per the schedule.
9. *Speak clearly:* While taking the classes the trainer must be clear in his expression and must use simple and understandable language to the trainees. He must also observe whether the trainees are able to follow his class without any difficulty.
10. *No arguments with the trainees:* A trainer should not enter into arguments with the trainees inside the class. During several occasions, some trainees who are knowledgeable would like to pose difficult questions to the trainer. On such occasions the trainer must patiently replay the trainees.

Manager as the Trainer

Managers, very many times may become an effective trainer. They have the added advantage of work experience to be combined with that of a trainer. They face work-based training opportunities everyday. Managers have their own work to complete as well as managing their team. This involves maintaining their professional practice and keeping in touch with the process that they manage as well as dealing with communications with other parts of the organization. Managers are also responsible for training and development of their employees. They are the right people to identify the training needs of their employees. Through their managing of operations they can monitor on a day-to-day basis the matching of tasks with competencies. A manager to be a trainer should have the skills of coaching, delegating, mentoring, work shadowing, and group development activities.

Supervisors as Trainers

Supervisors often do task related training themselves because it is most advantageous to them and to the worker being trained. Many supervisors have been elected for their position because of their superior knowledge of job content. They also know the individual workers and their needs. Supervisors who must train their employees might keep these pointers in mind:

- Have a clear, specific learning objective.
- Find out what employees know.
- Demonstrate as much as you are able.
- Encourage questions.
- Expect mistakes.
- Recognize accomplishments.
- Follow up frequently.

If supervisors cannot do the training themselves due to lack of time or expertise, they should be fully involved in the planning and selection of trainers and training programmes, for ultimately they are responsible for the workers in their group and its productivity. The trainers selected should fit these four criteria:

1. Understand thoroughly the knowledge, skills, or attitudes that must be taught.
2. Know how to teach those who will be learning.
3. Be willing and available at the time needed.
4. Be affordable.

A Supervisor's On-the-job Training Guide

1. *Prepare yourself*
    - Decide what must be taught at this time to meet an objective of improving safety, efficiency or quality.
    - Gather the right tools, equipment and materials, including enough for mistakes.
    - Arrange the teaching space to resemble the way the work space should be kept.
2. *Prepare the Learner*
    - Try to relax the tension—a little humor never hurt anyone
    - Explain why the person is being taught.
    - Create interest and encourage questions by asking what the learner already knows about this job.
    - Give an overview of the workplace and what is in it.
    - Explain the whole job and how this relates to other work the trainee already knows.
    - Put the learner as close to the normal working position as possible.
    - Familiarize the learner with the terms, equipment, tools, or materials to be used.
3. *Presentation of the operation*
    - Explain the quality and quantity requirements.

- Demonstrate the job at the normal pace.
- Demonstrate the job more slowly, stopping between steps in the operation, invite questions.
- Explain the key points and where errors are most likely to occur.
- Have the learner explain the steps as you go through them slowly.
- Have the learner explain the key points as you go through the steps slowly.

4. *Practice*
   - Have the learner try the job explaining each step to you.
   - Correct mistakes if necessary and try again.
   - Do some of the harder steps a few times if necessary.
   - You, the trainer, run the job at a normal pace.
   - Have the learner do the job, gradually building up speed.
   - When the trainee can do the job, let the person work on his or her own.
   - Don't abandon the learner.
5. *Follow-up*
   - Tell the learner who will be available for help or to answer question if necessary.
   - Gradually decrease supervision, checking against quality and quantity standards.
   - Correct faulty methods before they become a habit by showing why the learned method is better.

Compliment good work and continue encouragement to meet quality and quantity standards.

What fundamental should new trainers know?

Focus on these four factors in any train—the trainer programme

1. *Task analysis:* The new trainer be able to break down a task into parts that can easily conveyed in the classroom or other training situation.

2. *Lesson plan preparation:* The trainer learns to present material in logical progression, to cover the right amount of material, to review key points, etc.
3. *Presentation skills:* Videotaped presentations are played back for the participants so that they can learn from their mistakes. They are also valuable feedback from the others in the train—the trainer programme.
4. *Audio-visuals:* These are an important aspect of effective training. The new trainers learn the fundamentals of creating good learning aids.

Trainer Effectiveness

Trainer's Appearance

A trainer should look like a professional. Firstly, the trainer should dress according to the type of instruction being giving, and to whom it's being given.

A trainer should also look organized. If you're going into a classroom, have your material in a neat and organized pile, with the things you want to use first placed on top, and then work down into the stack.

Where should a trainer stand?

If you are going to stand while you present the session, you should stand in front of the group. However, if you stand too till you can lose the group's attention, so move around a little, not too much, just enough to keep the participants watching you.

Don't try to hide yourself behind the chair, desk, overhead projector. This can create a barrier to your communication and therefore to learning. Stand in or to the side of any equipment, so that the participant can see all of you if they want to.

If you stand in front of your training aids you must ensure that everyone in the group can see around you. If they can't, your body has become a physical and mental barrier to learning. Also the participants may not let you know that you are obscuring their view; it is up to you to notice.

Communicating with Trainees

A good trainer can read the trainees by body language, by looking at the participants faces you can usually tell if they do not understand what the instruction is about. You must also be aware that the trainees can read your body language, so don't stand in front of the group with your arms folded and then tell them that you're open to questions.

It's also important for the trainer not to interrupt a trainee who is talking to them. A trainee who is cut off may tend to keep quiet after that insult. Obviously there are times when you do have to cut short a trainee who talks too much. If you don't, it can interfere with your communication to the whole group.

For effective communication to continue, the trainer must offer positive reinforcement to the participants during the session. This means acknowledging responses from the group to encourage more interaction. If you ignore any responses, you are likely to lose interaction. Sometimes, a particular member may stop contributing after being ignored, even if they have the information you're after.

Trainer must be lively, enthusiastic and full of vitality. If we can display these qualities, it motivates or interests the group. If the trainee is not motivated or interested in the instruction, learning may be very difficult if not impossible.

Communication does not have to mean verbal communication one hundred per cent of the time. Silent pauses during the instruction allow the main point to sink in. So you could plan to have some silent breaks during instruction immediately after the main points.

Gaining Attention by a Trainer

Humour may be used occasionally to gain the students' attention. When humour is used, the trainer must be certain that it is effective and appropriate.

The training must make certain that the topic of the joke is relevant to the training topic and that the story is not too long, as this can distract the participant. Humor must never be directed at any of the trainees, must never use religion, must not refer to any nationality and must never be directed specifically at one sex. These rules ensure that no one in the group is offended. If you offend one person in the class the whole group may close ranks against you.

To gain and keep the trainees' attention we need to use a variety of methods in our instruction. This means that we should use appropriate and relevant training aids where they fit into the session. We must also keep the trainees active and involved in the session.

By asking questions of the group we can be reasonably certain that we are gaining the participants' attention. If questions are being asked, not one wants to be the one who doesn't know the answer, so use this to your advantage. With this motivating technique, we need to follow a few rules. Keep the questions short and spread them around the group. Use 'overhead' type questions; that is, ask a question of the group, wait for a few seconds, and then nominate the participant who is to answer. This technique is sometimes referred to as the 'pose, pause and pounce' method of questioning. Remember to give the trainee praise for a correct answer. If you get an incorrect answer, get the group to help bring out the right answer.

Creating Interest

If visual aids are made by the trainer they must be made to attract, and keep, the trainees' interest. By writing legibly and neatly on the whiteboard you can keep the trainees' interest. If the writing is untidy or difficult to understand the trainees may just give up. If you're an untidy writer on the whiteboard, chalkboard or flip chart, take some time to practice so that you improve your style.

To create interest you can always link new material back to something the trainees are familiar with, that is relate new knowledge to previous knowledge.

Wherever possible, trainers should show that all of the subject matter relates to real-life situation. If trainees can see that the information may be of benefit to them, the trainer is creating interest.

Good Habits

Before moving on to a new area in the session, clean the whiteboard of old material and remove any other distractions such as samples or other training aids. Clean up the classroom before leaving, too. This will earn you some professional respect from the trainers in following sessions.

You should also be thoroughly prepared. This means having your objectives clearly stated, having the appropriate training methods selected, having a session plan and training aids prepared, and knowing where the spares are if anything burns out.

Seven ways to make sure participants remember your message:

1. Make them laugh.
2. Always use quizzes/questions.
3. Keep letting them know what's next.
4. Exercise the use of handouts.
5. Include tasks for them.
6. Tie it all together.
7. Follow up if necessary.

It's up to you as a professional trainer to encourage active learning and to create a learning atmosphere.

Eight tips from the very best trainers:

1. Please don't take yourself too seriously.
2. Remember to keep a glass of water handy.
3. Always put your best voice forward.
4. Check your posture, stand up straight.
5. Take time to build a relationship.
6. Include vocal breaks for yourself.
7. Change the pace as you go.
8. Encourage a conversational style.

Teaching

The ability to teach, is an attribute not possessed by all. It is extraordinarily difficult to transform an ordinary manager or training specialist into a lecturer, discussion leader, or coach. But a few general principles have emerged from research and practice that trainers can use to good advantage in the classroom or on the job. These principles, if constituently and carefully applied, help trainers facilitate learning by building on whatever ability and motivation trainees bring to the task.

The principles fall into the following general categories: goal setting, material presentation, practice, feedback, and classroom behaviour.

Goal Setting

Goals are powerful spurs to performance in training as well as other settings. They help cognitively because trainees know what is expected of them. They also help motivationally by energizing, directing, and sustaining effort toward their accomplishment. Instructional objectives can be communicated to trainees and, if accepted, can serve as their goals as well as the trainer's. Since instructional objectives may be seen as rather general and remote, trainers usually find it desirable as well to set sub goals along the way.

Research suggests that instructional objectives (or sub-goals) are most effective in enhancing performance when they are specific and challenging. Challenging objectives are those that stretch the abilities of the trainees but are not so difficult that they are seen as impossible to reach and thus not worth striving for. Setting challenging sub-goals for trainees are a challenging sub goal for trainers.

Material Presentation

Material should be presented to trainees in the way that will be most meaningful and easily understood. The trainer can take a giant step in this direction at the outset of a programme and the beginning of each sub-part by providing trainees with an overview of the material to be learned. This helps to highlight goals (or sub-goals) and to tie the pieces of the material together. Then the material should be presented in a logical order, recognizing that the trainer may not totally control this when discussion and other participative training techniques are used.

Practice

A key to learning is practice. Practice enables trainees to shape appropriate responses to behaviours in an environment where mistakes are not too costly.

How much practice is enough? Available evidence suggests that there can be both too much and too little, but that the right amount varies from situation to situation. For most tasks, it is probably sufficient to continue practice until trainees are able to demonstrate satisfactory levels of performance several times within tolerable limits of error. For tasks that are encountered only infrequently on the job, are performed under stressful conditions, and are critical, trainers use the concept of over learning. That is, they continue practice far beyond the point of ordinary proficiency. The purpose of this is to build up such a strong stimulus-response connection in the trainees, 'minds that the learned skills will be invoked almost automatically.

Feedback

In training, feedback is important to performance because it helps keep learning on track and because it can serve as a form of reward or punishment to foster motivation. This is particularly true in self-paced, as opposed to externally paced, learning environments. Some feedback comes from the learning task itself as practice is successfully carried out and goals and sub-goals are attained. Other feedback comes from the trainer and/or fellow trainees in the form of verbal instructions, praise, or criticism. Both positive and negative feedback should be as specific as possible to clarify expectations and eliminate ambiguity. Verbal feedback should be provided as soon as practicable after the act that is being acknowledged.

Experienced trainers point out that great individual differences in the need for verbal feedback usually exist in any group of trainees. Some seem to adjust their behaviours and maintain their motivation with only task feedback, and others require considerable feedback from the trainer.

Classroom Behaviour

In classrooms trainers should behave in a professional manner, employing the best available training techniques and teaching methods and treating trainees fairly and ethically. Many observers believe that trainers should think of themselves as models for trainees by demonstrating desired behaviours whenever possible, working hard to eliminate annoying habits that retard learning, and developing a repertoire of knowledge and skills that can be brought to bear in varying situations almost on demand.

Work-based Training Opportunities

1. *Coaching*

   Coaching can be described as helping or enabling an individual or a small group in the workplace to acquire knowledge or develop a skill, which are needed to improve the job performance. A manager can use coaching for:

   (a) Skills development, such as using a software package.

   (b) Performance development such as work assignments.

   (c) Behavioural development, such as working with a colleague.

   In addition to the above, the managers have to develop the following:

(a) Listening skills to establish what the learner already knows and assess how motivated they are to learn.

(b) Facilitation skills to help keep the focus of the learner.

(c) Instructional skills to make clear presentations.

(d) Challenging skills to help the leaner to reassess performance.

(e) Feedback skills to enable the learner to develop their own sense of doing.

(f) Assessing skills to test understanding and performance.

2. *Delegation*

Delegation creates excellent opportunity for managers to provide structured learning to their staff. Effective delegation also makes a major statement to staff about the levels of trust that exist in the organization. The skills that managers need to develop to use delegation as a training opportunity include:

(a) *Task assessment:* What competencies does the task call for? How important is the work?

(b) *Person assessment:* Who has the potential to handle the work?

(c) *Contracting:* Drawing up a clear set of objectives, lines of responsibility, and deadlines for the work.

(d) *Giving feedback:* When to intervene? How to do it in a positive way?

(e) *Assessing:* Reviewing the delegated task outcomes and the process the person used to achieve them.

3. *Mentoring*

Mentoring can be described as "an agreement between an experienced and a less experienced colleague, where the more experienced provides help and support to improve the mentee's job performance". Mentoring can provide continuing and customized support for the members of the team. The manager's main role in mentoring are:

(a) To identify situations where mentoring is feasible and desirable.

(b) To explain the mentoring scheme to participants and prepare them to get the most benefit.

(c) To help mentee define the type of help they are looking for.

(d) To help them identify suitable mentors in other parts of the organization.

(e) To monitor the progress and outcomes of the scheme.

Mentoring schemes may be set up for staff who are taking new responsibilities or who need specific support to handle difficult assignments.

4. *Work shadowing*

   Work shadowing is an effective way of doing good practices within the organization. Placing a new or inexperienced person for a while with someone who performs well should create plenty of opportunity for learning on-the-job. They need to select the staff who will be shadowed, not just for their expertise but for the willingness to help a less experienced person. It is important that the purpose of the work shadowing is fully discussed and agreed between all parties, so that an informal contract can be drawn up.

5. *Group development activities*

   As the manager acquires the role of a trainer, he can begin to make constructive use of the occasions when staff works together. Making such events more interactive and more focused on everyone's learning will help establish greater trust and understanding. People who have been attending training courses can make presentations supported by good ideas they picked up. Project work also has its own way of use for group discussion.

6. *Training at the desk or in the learning center*

   With the advent of web-based communications, training is now being made available to staff at their workplace. All the advantages of multimedia and computer-based training can now be delivered online to work-based learners. Managers who wants to use this type of learning as part of their training strategy will need to:

   (a) Find a good source of web-based material.

(*b*) Select programmes that match most closely organizational and departmental development goals.

(*c*) Ensure that their IT networks and PCs have the capacity to handle online material.

(*d*) Induce their staff in this way of learning.

(*e*) Monitor the progress.

Summary

- Trainers Training programmes are required to be organized for equipping trainers. They have to be trained first.
- Trainers play a crucial role in training programmes. We can have managers as trainers, supervisors as trainers.
- There are work-based training opportunities to improve the competency of the staff members.

Self-Learning Activity

Try to answer the following questions on your own:

1. Why do we need TOT?
2. What is mentoring?
3. What is the role of trainers?

17

Estimation of Training Costs

While estimating the training cost the following factors are to be considered.

1. *Comforts:* As trainees come from various parts of the country they should be provided with minimum comforts. Comforts are relating to adequate accommodation, well furnished classrooms, reasonable food, recreation facilities, etc. The cost should bear these facts in mind.
2. *Training atmosphere:* A conducive atmosphere in the training place must be created. This is possible by way of creating friendly attitude with the fellow trainees, a cordial atmosphere with the trainers and providing minimum required physical facilities noted above.
3. *Mutual exchange of ideas:* The trainees must be given an opportunity to exchange each other's views and respect every ones' viewpoints. As the training unit consists of people of varied experiences, certainly new experiences and unique experience may come from the trainees. A forum must be created during the training hours to have separate session for discussions.
4. *Learning new knowledge and techniques:* One of the objectives of training is to inculcate new knowledge and techniques to the trainees. Such new knowledge and techniques may

be related to sophisticated training equipments or through latest computer languages. Such things may have greater bearing on the cost of training.

5. *Evaluation:* At the end of a training period evaluation is done. An evaluation must be made compulsory and the training unit must prepare proper evaluation tools quite prior to the training sessions.

Cost Areas

The cost areas for training is classified under two heads, namely, fixed costs and variable costs. Fixed cost is one where investment is made on the permanent assets. Such investment is made one time. Variable costs vary according to the type of facilities we provide to the trainees.

Fixed Cost

1. *Land and buildings:* This is the basic investment and a fixed cost that is to be managed by a training center. Proper planning is needed to purchase land and construct buildings, which are costlier.
2. *Furniture:* A training unit needs latest furniture to provide physical comforts to the trainees. Investment on this can be made gradually depending on the number of training programmes and number of trainees to be accommodated.
3. *Equipments:* A training unit needs number of equipments, which must be costly and latest one. Investment on computers, audio-visual aids, power point projectors, etc. are very much needed in a training center.
4. *Vehicles:* These are mobile assets, which may be treated as fixed costs. Vehicles are needed to provide transport arrangement to the trainees as wells as to the trainers and to bring guest faculties. Transport arrangement is needed to take the trainees to various places like tourist spots and on-the-job-training units.
5. *Hostels:* An investment on hostel buildings is a must for a training center. Such hostel facilities should have comforts needed for the trainees and enough facilities must be made to bear summer, winter and other seasons.

Variable Cost

Variable costs are not standard one and they may vary from period to period. They are as follows:

1. *Salary:* While planning the cost of training the salary to be paid to the trainers and supporting staff must be taken into consideration. A separate budget must be provided for the salary throughout the year.
2. *Teaching aids:* An expenditure on teaching aids is necessary. A training center has to purchase teaching aids like audio-visual equipments, well furnished blackboards and such of the facilities.
3. *Recreation:* The trainees must be provided with recreation facilities and sports facilities to pass their evening and leisure times productively. Such facilities must be provided within the campus and nearer to the hostel.
4. *Health:* An inbuilt health facility must be arranged for the trainees. As they come from different parts of the country climatic changes and food habits may affect their health.
5. *Secretarial assistance:* At the training center the trainees must be provided with computer facilities and secretarial assistance. As they may have to prepare seminar papers and discussion materials, such assistance is very much needed.
6. *Library:* A well-built library with latest books and journals is a pre-requisite for an effective training. An investment on library is an asset to the training center.

Budget Preparation

While preparing the budget a training institute as well as the institute, which is deputing trainees, must prepare their own budgets. Here the budget preparation denotes the budget to be prepared by training centers. The following factors must be considered while preparing the budget.

1. *Fixed costs:* Enough money must be allocated for the fixed cost. The investment on fixed costs may be one time or gradual. Depending on that the cost of training may vary.

2. *Salary to the employees:* This is the most important expenditure to be kept in mind while preparing the budget and analyzing cost of training.
3. *Power/Electricity:* The training center must prepare a budget and an expenditure item for the power or electricity to be consumed by the training center.
4. *Fuel:* Fuel is another item that will decide the cost of training. The number of trips to be arranged and the number of trainees will decide the fuel cost.
5. *Stationary:* Stationeries like paper, computer inks, etc must be considered while calculating cost of training. Stationeries needed both for the trainees as well as the trainers.
6. *Catering:* As the trainees are to be given food and accommodation, the cost of such facilities must be calculated.

Period of Cost Calculation

The cost of training for the training institute can be calculated for various periods like monthly, quarterly, half-yearly and yearly. The training cost can also be calculated on the basis of the period of training, which may run to few days, few weeks or even few months.

Estimation of Training Costs

Apart from the budget preparation noted above, the following factors must be considered while estimating the training cost.

1. *Number of trainees:* The cost of a training programme is decided by the primary factor the number of trainees to be accommodated in a training programme. Higher the number of trainees, lower will be the training cost. But with higher number of trainees the quality of training may go down.
2. *Number of training programmes:* The cost of training that to be conducted by training center depends on the number of training programmes for a year. If more number of

training programmes are conducted, fuller utilization of faculties and facilities are made, which may bring down the training cost. On the other hand few training may increase the training cost.

3. *Duration of each training:* A training programme can be conducted for two, three days, a week, or few weeks or even for few months. Longer the duration, lower will be the cost of training. Shorter the duration, higher will be the cost of training.
4. *Guest lectures:* To make a training programme effective, guest lecturers must be invited and they must be exposed to the trainees. This may incur a cost, which is to be kept in mind while calculating the cost of training.
5. *Funds:* While calculating the training costs the collection of funds to meet the training cost must be calculated. Training centers may have their own funds through budgetary provisions; they may collect funds from other sources like government, open market and foreign agencies. Funds can also be collected from the sponsoring agencies who are sending trainees for training. In the case of cooperatives, cooperative training institutes collect money from the sponsoring institutions.

Identifying Training Costs/Indicators

There are certain additional factors to identify the training costs using the following indictors.

1. *Cost per day of training:* This compares the total expenditure on training per annum with the total number of days of training per annum. The resulting cost per day can be used as a guide in budgeting, as a comparison with the cost of external training and as a measure of trend in cost on a year to year basis.
2. *Average training days provided per trainee:* This compares the total number of training days provided per annum with the total number of employees. For example, a training range of 1 to 5 days per employee — multiply this figure

by the number of staff employed and the cost per day of training, the total budget allocation can be derived.

3. *Internal* vs *external training costs:* It is useful to compare regularly the cost per day of internal training with the average cost for one day of training from an external supplier.
4. *Training days delivered per trainer per annum:* This figure compares the total training days delivered for annum with the average number of training staff employed over the year. Such figures are affected by the number of events, the duration of the events, and the attendance at each event. However, it is necessary to estimate each of these variables when producing the budget. The plan itself will include elements such as computer-based training, educational courses, and other training approaches.

The actual preparation of the budget requires the following steps.

1. Identify what elements of the plan will follow on from the previous year.
2. Identify what new initiatives will be required to meet the business plan.
3. Determine what training methods and approaches will be used.
4. Specify what volumes of activity will be required.
5. Identify how the employee development will be delivered. E.g., training courses, CBT, action learning, and what resources will be required, e.g., training rooms, technology-based resources, etc.
6. Convert this data to financial statements under appropriate cost headings.
7. Provide narrative justification for the budget identifying contribution to the business plan together with a clear statement of the cost involved using appropriate accounting conventions.

8. Convince the senior management of the merits of the case in the budget.

Assessing the Cost and Benefits of Training

A variety of methods can be used to assess the value of training. Two of that are increasingly being used by psychologists are calculations of ROI and Utility analysis.

No matter which approach is used, costs and benefits associated with training must be estimated. Some costs that should be measured for a training programme include:

1. One-time cost such as needs assessment cost, salaries and media (computer, videos, handouts, distance learning techniques). Programme development costs, evaluation cost for the first offering of the programme.
2. Costs associated with each training session such as trainers' costs (e.g. salaries and benefits, travel, lodging. Meals) and facilities rental.
3. Costs associated with trainees including trainee wages during training. Lodging, and meals for trainees during travel.

It is important to compare the benefits of training programme with its costs. One benefit that should be estimated is the money payback associated with the improvement in trainees' performance after receiving training. This is often difficult to approximate. Since the results of the experimental design will indicate any differences in behaviour between those untrained. The trainer can then estimate for that particular group of employees (e.g., managers, engineers) what this difference is worth in terms of the salaries of those employees. Often, the amount gained per trainee per year is multiplied by the number of persons trained. Another factor that should be considered when estimating the benefits of training is the duration of the training's impact: that is, the length of time during which the improved performance will be maintained. While probably no programmes will show benefits forever, those that do incur longer-term improved performance will have greater value to the organization.

Return on Investment (ROI)

Given the increasing amount of money that firms budget on training, it is imperative that companies be able to estimate the return on investment (ROI) that training provides them. To do this, firms should assess the costs and benefits associated with their programmes. In one study of several training programmes at a pharmaceutical firm it was found that the managerial training programmes had an average ROI of 45 per cent, while the sales and technical training programmes had an average ROI of 156 per cent. At Ford, all training programmes are evaluated against the criterion of product line profitability. A tracking system shows costs and revenue for training facilities and individual courses. The basic ROI formula is as follows:

$$\text{ROI}(\%) = \frac{\text{Net programme benefit} \times 100}{\text{Programme costs}}$$

For example, at an 18-week literacy programme for entry level electrical and mechanical assemblers at Magnavox Electronics Systems Company, the results were impressive. The benefits (productivity and quality) were \$321,600 while the costs were only \$38,233. Thus, the ROI is calculated as 741 per cent. This means that for each dollar invested, Magnavox received \$7.41 over the cost of the programme.

$$\text{ROI}=\frac{\$321,600 - \$38,233 \times 100}{\$38,233} = 741\%$$

When making ROI calculations, it is important to use reliable and credible sources and to be conservative when estimating benefits and costs for training. It is also important to involve management when deciding on what is an acceptable ROI as a target goal for the training. For example, British Airways has utilized training to become one of the most profitable airlines in the world. Before training begins, a tangible value for the training investment is set; reflecting how much improvement in customer satisfaction is to be expected if training is successful.

Utility Analysis

Another approach that can be used when calculating the value of training is a utility model. This is difficult but may be important for showing top management the value of training for the organization. Utility analysis measures the economic contribution of a programme according to how effective it was in identifying and modifying behaviour.

Because the calculations involved in a utility analysis are based on subjective estimations, this model has not yet gained widespread acceptance by trainers as a practical tool for evaluating return on training investments.

Designs for Evaluating Training

After determining the criteria to be used in evaluating the training programme, the trainer should choose an experimental design. The design is used to answer two primary questions:

1. whether or not a change has occurred in the criteria (e.g, learning, behaviour, organizational results); and
2. whether or not the change can be attributed to the training programme.

Designs employ two possible strategies to answer these questions.

The first is to compare the trainee's performance before and after participation in training. This is done to see what changes may have occurred in learning, behaviour, or organizational results. While this is important for answering the question of whether change has taken place, it is deficient in answering the question of whether the change can be attributed to the training programme since the criteria may have changed for a number of reasons. Answering the second question requires a design comparing the changes that occurred in the trainees with change that occurred in another group of employees who did not receive the training (e.g., a control group), yet are similar to the training group in important ways (e.g., similar job titles, rank, geographical location). The most effective experimental designs use both strategies (i.e.; before and after measures and a control group) and are better able to answer both questions. Some of the more commonly used designs for training evaluation are described below:

One-Shot posttest-Only Design

In many organizations, training is designed and conducted without prior thought given to evaluation. For example, a plant manager may decide to put all the employees in a safety training. After the course is completed, the manager decides to evaluate it. At this point, the design would look like the one below:

TRAINING ⟶ MEASURE

Any of the four types of criteria (e.g., reactions, learning, behaviour, organizational results) could be used as the "after" measures. It would be difficult, however, to know what, if any, changes occurred since no "before" measure (e.g., pretest) was made. In addition, because the results may not be compared with those of another group who did not receive training, it would not be possible to say whether any change was due to the training. If, however, the primary goal was to make sure that the trainees reached a certain mastery level, then the design might still be appropriate (e.g., the trainees reached a 95 per cent safety goal).

One-Group Pretest-Posttest Design

Another design for evaluating the training group on the criteria is to measure the group before and after the training. This design is as follows:

MEASURE ⟶ TRAINING ⟶ MEASURE

This design can assess whether a change has occurred for the training group in the criteria (e.g., learning, behaviour) that is useful. Unfortunately, it is not able to tell for sure whether or not the change is due to training, since there is no control group. A change that is detected could have been caused by the introduction of new equipment, a new manager, revised pay systems, or a number of other reasons. If the trainee is going to use this design, it is important to document other events that have occurred during the measurement period to determine the most likely explanations for any detected changes.

Posttest- only Control Group Design

A much stronger design for assessing the effectiveness of a training programme is shown here:

GROUP 1: R: TRAINING ------- MEASURE

GROUP 2: R: NO TRAINING------- MEASURE

In this design, two groups are used and individuals are randomly assigned (R) to either group (i.e. an individual has an equal chance of being put in either group 1— the training group, or group 2— the control group). The use of random assignment helps to initially equalize the two groups. This is important to ensure that any differences between the two group after training are not simply caused by difference in ability, motivation, or experience. The posttest only control group design is useful when it is difficult to collect criteria measures on individuals prior to offering them the training. For example, the trainer may believe that giving individuals a pretest, such as a learning test, may overly influence their scores on the posttest, which might be the same learning measure. Another trainer may not have time to give pre-measures, individuals are randomly assigned to the two groups, and their scores on the posttest are compared. Any difference on the posttest can be attributed to the training programme since we can assume the two group were somewhat equal before training. It would be beneficial to make sure the employees from the control group are placed in a training programme later so that they have similar opportunities.

Pretest-Posttest Control Group Design

Another powerful design that is recommended for use in training evaluation is as follows:

GROUP 1: R MEASURE ⟶
TRAINING ⟶ MEASURE
GROUP 2: R MEASURE ⟶
NO TRAINING ⟶ MEASURE

Individual are randomly assigned to the two groups. Criteria measures are collected on both groups before and after the training programme is offered, yet only one group actually receives the training (Group 2 is the control group). Comparisons are made of the changes detected in both groups. If the change in Group 1 is significantly different than the change in Group 2, we can be somewhat certain that it was caused by the training. The two features that make this a stronger design are the randomization of people into the groups, and the use of a control group. These aspects enable us to determine:

1. if a change occurred; and
2. whether the change was due to training.

Since many organizations will want all of the employees in both groups to receive the training, the training can be offered to Group 2 at a later time.

Multiple times design

Another design recommended for use in training evaluation is shown below:

GROUP 1: R
MEASURE ⟶ MEASURE ⟶ MEASURE ⟶
TRAINING ⟶ MEASURE ⟶ MEASURE ⟶
MEASURE ⟶

GROUP 2: R
MEASURE ⟶ MEASURE ⟶ MEASURE ⟶
NO MEASURE ⟶
MEASURE ⟶ MEASURE ⟶ MEASURE

In this design, individuals are randomly assigned to either of two groups, and the criteria measures (learning, behaviour, results) are collected at several times before and after the training has been offered. This design allows us to observe any changes between the two groups over time or any trends in performance. If the effects of training held up over several months, this design would offer stronger support for the programme. Of course, this design might be more costly or difficult to implement since it requires taking measurements of individuals multiple times.

Benchmarking Training Efforts

To conduct a thorough evaluation of a training programme, training departments can benchmark their practices against the best in the industry. They can compare their training department to leading-edge companies in terms of:

1. *Training activities* (e.g., per cent of payroll spent on training. Average training hours per employee, training dollars spent per employee, per cent of employees trained per year, training staff per 1000 employees);
2. *Training results* (e.g., average per cent of positive trainee ratings per year, average per cent of satisfied trainees, average per cent gain in learning per course, average per cent of improvement in job performance, cost savings as a ratio of training expenses, revenues per employee per year. Profits per employee per year); and
3. *Training efficiency* (e.g., training costs per student hour, time on task). The American Society for Training and Development (ASTD) established a benchmarking service in 1997 available to all organizations around the world that want to assess the strengths and weaknesses of their training services.

Transfer of Training

The ultimate goal of a training programme is that the learning that occurs during training be transferred back to the job. To maximize transfer, the following suggestions have been offered. These include ideas for the training session itself as well as for the employee once he or she has returned to the job:

1. Maximize the similarity between the training context and the job context. That is, the training should resemble the job as closely as possible.
2. Require practice of the new behaviours and over learning in training.
3. Encourage trainees to practice skills on their jobs in between training sessions.
4. Include a variety of stimulus situations in the practice so that trainees will learn to generalize their knowledge and skills.
5. Label or identify the important features of the content to be learned to distinguish the major steps involved.
6. Develop, and have available on the job, job aids to reminded employees of the key action steps necessary on the job.
7. Make sure that the general principles underlying the specific content are understood in training.
8. Ensure that there is a supportive climate for learning and for transferring new behaviours. This can be done by building managerial support (emotional and financial) for training, providing trainees with the freedom to set personal performance goals, and encouraging risk-taking among trainees.
9. Build the trainee's self-efficacy for learning and using the new skills. Self-efficacy is a feeling of control and accomplishment; that you can control your own destiny.
10. Once back on the job, employees should be given opportunities to demonstrate that they can use the new skills.
11. Encourage continual learning by employees. They should realize that one-time training in an area is not sufficient to maintain effective skills. Retraining also may be needed to update skills.

Note: This part of the chapter has been drawn from the book *Human Resource Management—Experimental Approach* by John Bernardin, Tata McGraw Hill, 2004.

Summary

- There are certain factors that are to be considered in the estimation of training cost.
- While preparing budget for training also the organization has to consider some factors.
- There are certain ways to assess cost benefit of training in an organization. The evaluators should employ such measures to assess the training cost benefits.

Self-Learning Activity

Try to answer the following questions on your own:

1. What are the factors to be considered in estimating training cost?
2. Discuss budget preparation for training.
3. How do you assess cost-benefit of training?

18

EVALUATION OF TRAINING

Definition

"It is an attempt to obtain information (feedback) on the effects of a training programme and to assess the value of the trainee in the light of the information".

Why Evaluation?

Evaluation of trainee is needed for the following reasons.

1. *To make the training programme effective:* To make any training programme effective a system of evaluation is needed. Through evaluation we can examine the various methods of teaching, content of the lessons, training environment, etc.
2. *It is used as a training aid:* Once an evaluation is made, it becomes a full proof method of a training programme, which will be useful for subsequent training programmes. It forms a basis to revise the training materials and forms an important training aid.
3. *To verify whether goals are achieved against targets:* Every training programme as well as the organizations fixes goals for the training programme. Targets are also fixed in terms of budget, quality of training, period of training, content of training, etc. Such goals must be measured against the targets fixed above, for which evaluation is very much needed.

4. *Cost effectiveness achieved or not:* Through an evaluation system the benefits of a training programme, to the organization as well as to the trainees can be assessed by means of verifying cost-effectiveness of the training programme. That means the money spent on training must be fruitful and useful in terms of producing efficiency, improvement in work, new procedures, etc.
5. *To find useful to the individuals and the organization:* A training evaluation must pave the way for effective utilization thereby resulting in benefits to the organization as well as to the individuals.

Objectives of Evaluation

Training evaluation has the following objectives to the trainers, trainees and to the organization.

1. *Reliable indicator to verify the effectiveness of training:* Only a training evaluation can be made a reliable indicator to verify the effectiveness of a training programme. No other method can be called to the method of training evaluation.
2. *To check whether identified priorities have been well targeted:* Any training programme must have objectives and priorities, which are to be fixed. Through evaluation we can find whether priorities mentioned earlier have been well targeted and achieved to the satisfaction of all the concerned.
3. *To improve the methods of work:* An evaluation will make a training programme effective by means of inculcating new knowledge and efficiency to the trainees. These things must guarantee improvement in the methods of work that is to be discharged by the trainees.
4. *To make the process like transfer and promotion easier:* A training evaluation is one of the indicators to evaluate the involvement, participation and efficiency of an employee in the training programme as well as in the organizational work. So training evaluation will make the transfer and

promotion job easier for the organization, because through evaluation we can find the individuals improvement in work.

5. *Improve the training process:* An evaluation will make the training process broader and useful to all the people concerned. An evaluation will tell what to add and what to delete during the next round of training.
6. *To update and refresh old employees:* As training is a continuous process for the employees, all employees must be given training at all levels and stages. An evaluation at this stage will make the organization to understand whether the senior employees are able to keep themselves abreast with the changing organizational goals and organizational dynamics.
7. *To enhance production and reduce wastage:* Any training programme must work towards increasing the efficiency of the employees. An evaluation can verify whether such training programmes are productive and improve the efficiency of the trainees as well as reduce wastages in the workplace.
8. *Acts as feedback to the organization on training:* Organizations depute employees for training spending their own money. Naturally, they will be curious to know whether that money spent on training have been used productively. An evaluation can act as feedback to know the utility of training.
9. *It raises the commitment and involvement of trainees during training:* An evaluation can make the trainees to understand their commitment to the training and their active participation in the training programmes.
10. *To enable people to work with minimum supervision and wastage:* Supervision has become the order of the day in organizations, which involves a considerable amount of expenditure. An effective training and a training evaluation helps an organization to know how far supervision can be minimized wastages could be avoided.

11. *It helps an individual on where he stands in grasping and performance:* A training evaluation can help an individual to understand his grasping power and the performance that he had done during the training period.

Timing of Training Evaluation

Training evaluation can be made during three periods, namely, before the training, during the training and after the completion of training.

Before the Training

1. *To know whether the selected training methods were useful:* When a training evaluation is made before the training, we can come to know whether the selected training methods were useful or not. Accordingly we can add new things or eliminate the unwanted one.
2. *Have other trainees used this method and successful?* Through evaluation, when it is done before training we can come to know whether the previous trainees have used these methods successfully or not.
3. *Test the methods over highly skilled employees:* When an evaluation is undertaking before the training, it can be administered over well-qualified employees and we can gather their opinion about various methods of training.
4. *Does the method suit the employees' preference and learning styles?* An evaluation before the training can help a training organization to know whether the employees preferred such methods and that suits the learning capacities and learning styles of the trainees.
5. *Difficulties faced in understanding various methods:* A training evaluation before the training can explain us the difficulties faced by the trainees in understanding various methods of training.

Evaluation during the Training

1. *Ask whether they are able to follow the programmes:* When an evaluation is undertaken during the training period, we can come to know whether the trainees are able to follow

the training programmes or not. Accordingly we can change the training programme to suit the needs of the trainees.

2. *Conduct short tests on programmes:* When evaluation is undertaken during the training period simple tests are administered over the trainees to understand the usefulness of training programmes.
3. *Do the trainees actively involve in the programmes?* An evaluation during the training period will make us to understand whether the trainees are actively involving themselves in the programmes. Otherwise, we can ask them their difficulties.

Evaluation after the Completion of Training

1. *Comparing the evaluation before the training and after the training:* By comparing the training programmes before and after the training, the results can be compared during the two periods and steps can be taken to rectify any shortfalls in the training.
2. *Interview the trainees before the training programme and compare the results:* By means of conducting an interview with the trainees before and after the training programme, we can compare the results of the training.
3. *Assign an expert evaluation from inside and outside:* While evaluating a training programme, the evaluation team must contain an expert within the training center and outside the training center. This will make the impartial assessment of training evaluation.

Contents of an Evaluation Tool

An evaluation tool must contain the following matters:

1. *It should be simple:* Any training evaluation tool prepared must be easily understandable to the trainees and evaluators.
2. *It must cover prominent areas:* The evaluation tool must contain questions on prominent areas like various training methods, trainers, place of training, facilities, etc.

3. *Pre-test it:* Before an evaluation tool is administered, it must be pre-tested, so that any unwanted questions can be removed.
4. *Impartial evaluation:* An evaluation tool must be prepared in such a way that it is impartial in nature and will not lead to biases.
5. *Evaluation by two experts:* An evaluation must be made by two experts internally and externally.
6. *Send the report to concerned people:* After the evaluation is over the report should be sent to the organization so that effective remedial arrangement can be made.

Steps involved in the Process of Evaluation

1. *Define what you aim to achieve through training:* While evaluating a training programme, the evaluators must understand about what they want to achieve through training programmes.
2. *Frame objectives out of targets:* Objectives and targets must be fixed for training evaluation. It is known as PARTS — Ponderable, Achievable, Realistic, Timely, Specific.
3. *Make sure that everyone is aware of the objectives:* The people who are concerned with training (trainer, trainee, training center and the organization) must understand the nature of evaluation.
4. *Evolve schemes and ways for comparing results with objectives:* While preparing the evaluation tool provision must be made comparing the results with each objective laid down.
5. *Appraise the inputs:* The evaluation should result in comparing the outcome of the evaluation with that of the expectations.
6. *Interpretation and application of results:* After collecting data, when the evaluation report is to be ready, it should be interpreted impartially so that the people concerned can know the true results of the evaluation.

CIRO Framework of Evaluation

One of the most common ways of evaluating management training is named CIRO Framework of Evaluation. CIRO stands for Context, Input, Reaction, and Outcome.

(a) *Context evaluation:* Obtaining and using information about the current operational context, that is, about individual difficulties, organizational deficiencies, and so on. In practice, this mainly implies the assessment of training needs as a basis for decision.

(b) *Input evaluation:* Obtaining and using information about possible training resources in order to choose between alternative inputs to training.

(c) *Reaction evaluation:* Obtaining and using information about trainees on expressed current or subsequent reactions in order to improve training.

(d) *Outcome evaluation:* Monitoring the consequences of training. Three levels of outcome evaluation may be distinguished.

1. *Immediate outcomes:* Changes in trainees' knowledge, skills and attitudes, which can be identified immediately after the completion of training. Assessment involves some measures of how people have changed during a training programme.
2. *Intermediate outcomes:* The changes in trainees' actual work behaviour, which result from training. Assessment involves monitoring performance on the job.
3. *Long-term outcomes:* The changes in the functioning of part or all of the organization, which have resulted from changes in work behaviour originated in training. Assessment is usually in terms of output or financial measures.

Criteria for Evaluation

There are three types of criteria for evaluating training-Internal, external and participant reaction.

Internal criteria are directly associated with the content of the programme. For example it is to know whether the employee learned the guidelines covered in the programme.

External criteria are related to the ultimate purpose of the programme. E.g., improving the effectiveness of the employee. The external criteria include job performance rating, degree of learning transferred from training to on the job situations, etc.

Participant reaction includes the benefits of a training programme.

Kirkpatrick Multiple Criterion Evaluation

The multiple criterion evaluation developed by Kirkpatrick explains the following criteria:

1. *Participant reaction:* The likes and dislikes of the participants are measured and the satisfaction of the participants towards training programme is also measured.
2. *Learning:* The extent to which the trainees have grasped the knowledge of and skills practiced in the training programme.
3. *Behaviour:* The change in the behaviour of the trainee before and after training.
4. *Results:* The effect of the training on organizational dimensions such as employee turnover, productivity, volume of sales, etc.

Evaluation Methods

1. *Company records* – Either existing records or those devised for the evaluation of training/development, used to measure production turnover, grievances, absenteeism, etc.
2. *Observational technique* – Interviewing, field observation and other methods to evaluate skills, ability, communication and productivity.
3. *Critical incidents* – Using critical incidents that occur on the job.

4. *Ratings* – Judgments of ability, performance/ratings of satisfaction with various factors.
5. *Questionnaires* – A variety of types to measure decision making, problem solving, attitudes, values, personality, perceptions, etc.
6. *Tests* – Written examinations to measure changes in ability or knowledge.

Levels of Evaluation

Evaluation is undertaken at four levels.

1. ***Reaction level***

At this stage the reactions of the trainees to various training methods are assessed (form opinions and attitude about the trainer, the method of presentation, the usefulness and the interest of the subject matter, their own involvement, etc.).

Reactions can be measured by rating scales, which will help to decide what to do next. Information on long-term reactions to training can be obtained through questionnaires or interview.

2. ***Learning level***

This is to know whether the trainees have learned new knowledge, skill, attitude and subject matter. 'Knowledge learning' can be evaluated by various forms of tests and examinations. The purest form of evaluation of knowledge learning is that used in programmed instructions, where knowledge is evaluated at every stage of the learning process. Even if programmed learning is not used, it is possible to construct tests consisting of multiple choice questions, which can be administered at the end of the training programme. Examinations of academic type can also be used to evaluate knowledge. Examinations need not be written, it can be oral. With regard to 'skill learning' can also be evaluated by tests, though in this case, they must be practical tests in which the trainee is given opportunity to demonstrate his skill.

Here, the test must be performed at the beginning and at the end of the training in order to measure the change effected by the training. With regard to 'attitude learning', attitude scales can be used. 'Semantic differential scales' (SD scales) can provide an effective approach. In this technique the trainees are given a sheet at the top of which the subject matter of the training is stated and below this are a number seven point or five point scales. Trainees are asked to rate the subject matter of the training on each of these scales. They must do it at the beginning and at the end of the training programme.

3. ***Job behaviour level***

This is to know whether the training has changed the behaviour of the employees when he joins back the job. It is also to know whether trainees have applied their learning in the form of changed behaviour on the job. A variety of evaluation techniques can be used, but the most important thing is the trainers should "get their feet wet", in other words, they should actively involve themselves to the job situation of their trainees, so that they obtain a large amount of unsystematic information about their job behaviour. The following are the techniques used here:

- *Activity sampling*– For discovering the percentage of time spent by the trainee on different aspects of his job, and observer diaries for obtaining a continuous record of the trainees' pattern of activities.
- *Self diaries* are another technique where the trainee keeps a record of his own activities over a specified period, often by ticking the appropriate columns on a pre-designed form at frequent intervals.
- Another technique used in job behaviour level is *observation of specific incidents*; here the evaluator or the trainer observes the trainee's performance during a specific incident relating to the subject matter of training.

- *Self-recording of specific incidents* is another devise through which the trainee can himself record the details in which he performs certain incident.
- Through *appraisal by superiors,* the seniors will ask descriptions of the job behaviour. The last technique is *self-appraisal,* which is a variation of appraisal which can be used along with other methods.

4. ***Functionuing level***

   It is for the organization to decide whether the training has resulted in cost-effective methods and to know the costs are worth for the training. Evaluation at this level consists of attempts to measure the job behaviour of the trainees (whether on the productivity or efficiency of the trainee's department, or on the morale of the subordinates, labor turnover rates or the incidents of industrial disputes).

Summary

- Training evaluation is an attempt to obtain information (feedback) on the effects of a training programme and to assess the value of the trainee in the light of the information.
- Evaluation as a tool should be used based on the requirements: before, during and after the training.
- There are criteria to evaluate training programmes: internal or external.

Self-Learning Activity

Try to answer the following questions on your own:

1. Why do organizations go for training evaluation?
2. What are the criteria for evaluating training?
3. List out the contents of evaluation tool.

19

EFFECTIVENESS OF TRAINING/TRANSFER OF TRAINING TO THE JOB

TRAINING EFFECTIVENESS

Training is the systematic modification of behaviour through learning that occurs as a result of education, instruction and development and planned experience. The fundamental aim of training is to help the organization achieve its purpose by adding value to its key resources — the people, its employee. Training means investing in people to enable them to perform better and to empower them to make the best use of their natural abilities.

The basic purpose of training is:

1. to increase productivity;
2. to increase quality;
3. to help a company fulfill its future personnel needs;
4. to improve organizational climate;
5. to improve health and safety;
6. obsolescence prevention;
7. personal growth, etc.

An effective training:

- Minimizes learning cost.
- Improves individual, team and corporate performance in terms of output, quality, speed and overall productivity.

- Improves operational flexibility by extending the range of skills possessed by the employees.
- Attracts high quality employees by offering them learning and development opportunities, increasing their levels of competence and enhancing their skills. Thus enabling them to obtain more job satisfaction to gain higher rewards and to progress within the organization.
- Increases the commitment of employees by encouraging them to identify with the mission and objectives of the organization.
- Helps to manage change by increasing understanding of the reasons for change and skills they need to adjust to new situation.
- Helps to develop a positive culture in the organization.
- Provides higher levels of service to customers.

Effectiveness

Traditionally, training development functions have been rather lax in the measurement of the effectiveness of training. However, with reduced budgets it is even more important to measure the effectiveness of the training. It is now well recognized that at the start of any initiative the success criteria should be identified and the outcomes reviewed against this criteria. The close the training and development matches the business needs, the more accurate the measures can become much more significant.

It is very important that evaluation of training should be regarded as an integrate part of the whole process of training and not as the last minute addition to make the training effective in real sense. A healthy approach is to adopt a policy that whenever a decision is taken to meet a training need, plans should also be drawn up to evaluate the same.

It is important to evaluate training in order to assess its effectiveness in producing the learning outcomes specified when the training intervention was planned and to indicate where improvements or changes are required to make the training even more effective.

Evaluating leads to control, which mean deciding whether or not the training was worthwhile and what improvement, are required to make it even more cost-effective. Evaluating is an integral feature of training. In its crudent form, it is the comparison of objectives with outcomes to answer the question of how far the training has achieved its purpose. The setting of objectives and the establishment of methods of measuring results are, or should be, an essential part of the planning stage of any training programme.

Why Evaluate?

(*a*) To know whether the course or session meets the objectives of the participants.
(*b*) To know whether the processes of the course were satisfactory.
(*c*) To find what participants think of speakers.
(*d*) To know whether the content was relevant.
(*e*) To discover how much laming has occurred.
(*f*) To know the impact of the course on the organization.
(*g*) To have data that can be used in preparing the marketing future raining.
(*h*) To try to estimate the cost-effectiveness of the training event, etc.

What to Evaluate?

(*a*) The learning processes.
(*b*) The teaching processes.
(*c*) Audio-visual aids.
(*d*) Content.
(*e*) The product.
(*f*) The premise and location.
(*g*) Accommodation or meals where residential training has been conducted.
(*h*) Long-term outcome in terms of the transference of skills to the workshop.
(*i*) Cost-effectiveness.

When training is external, then the training department should still evaluate the course and it might be wise to have specially prepared questions to be asked to the attendants.

How to Evaluate?

There are number of techniques used in evaluation, suchas:

1. ***Observation***

   This technique can be used, both during and after the training event, to look for evidence of learning and transfer of that learning to the way it provides a reasonable level of objectivity. The more unstructured the observation the higher risk of subjectivity creeping into the data.

2. ***Tests/Exams***

   A traditional method of assessment which is often used in written forms more for testing levels of knowledge and understanding that interpersonal skills. When used before or at the start of the training event, this methods can provide a benchmark. Later testing using similar instruments can demonstrate levels of improvement (or otherwise). Practical tests depend heavily on the skills of the examiner to spot the desired features. Some are:

   (a) *Achievement tests:* Shows what participants have learned or say they have learned and are fairly conclusive.

   (b) *Abiligy/aptitude tests:* Endeavors to show whether participants could undertake a particular task if asked to and gives good indication as to intellectual capability.

   (c) *Personaligy/Attitude Tests:* Attempts to show whether participants have the inclination to undertake a task.

3. ***Interviews***

   Interviewing is the traditional information-gathering tool of the researcher that enables the interviewer to explore a variety of situations such as: assessing people, gathering data, testing and sounding out ideas, obtaining people's opinions, etc. Therefore, a skilful interviewer gathers information effectively by encouraging the informant; formulating and asking focused questions while displaying appropriate non-verbal behaviour. Interviewing is a skill and there are no set rules to follow to guarantee a particular result. This is one of the weaknesses and also the strength of employing interviewing as an evaluation tool. There are basically three types of interviews, each method can be very effective depending on the result you are seeking and how much time and money you have got at your disposal:

(a) *Unstructured* or *open interview:* The interview is free ranging although within the boundaries of your research.

(b) *Structured interview:* The interview follows a preset path.

(c) *Semi-structured interview:* A mixture of the other two approacher.

4. ***Questionnaires***

They are targeted towards gathering information on how the respondents rate the importance and performance of specific aspects of their posts. It is important in order to avoid bias that where questionnaires are used, organizations use outside assistance in the formulation of the questionnaire and rating methodologies and/or in the coordination and analysis of the result.

5. ***Action plans***

These can be completed at the end of the training events as a form of remainder to participants about what they have learned and to place that in the context of their workplace. Although strictly speaking part of the transfer of learning, action plans can provide a very useful source of evaluation data. By analyzing action plans and later actual achievements, it is possible to measure change in a quantifiable way. Provided the action undertaken is within the context of the training events. Objectively, this method can provide a rich vein of information.

6. ***Learning logs***

   By encouraging participants to record their more significant learning or development points as they go through a training method and how the participant plans to transfer the learning back.

Suggestions

Suggestions for the organization and trainers to make training more effective are as follows:

1. *Plan the training with specific goals*

   The trainers should build the training around the identified needs for performance improvement. They should plan interventions to remove the barriers with the training. Ideally training must be supplemented with the changes, such as incentive systems, feedback systems, new recruitment methods, selection criteria, or other interventions. Include key persons as far as possible from the work unit participate in the training to enhance pre-reinforcement of new skills or behaviours. Ask trainee's manager to attend the training or a similar session to lead importance and secure their buy-in. Ask the manager to go back to his staff, describe the most important information, and ask them to describe how they can put that information into action. This critical dialogue is frequently missing.

2. *Define objectives and scope*

   When a manager initiates a request for training, ensure that he informs staff of the purpose of the training, and that all parties agree about goals and scope. Specific goal and a scope with stated boundaries will be important to the perceived success about the training. Managers must give the staff time for training and practice, they adjust their workloads or deadlines. Ensure that trainees know that the training will be put to good use.

3. *Reinforce and clarify expectations*

   Clarify expectations of what use is expected in the workplace of the training rather than assuming that the employee will use the training in the job. Remove any obstacle or job aids that obstruct the use of training to the job. Provide with the support that is needed at the workplace such as immediate superior, etc.

4. *Evaluate the outcome*

   Managers base evaluations on employee's demonstration of expected behaviours and skills. Plan, with trainer, a series of follow-up assessments requesting a copy of summary assessment documents. Evaluate the outcomes and expected results objectively. Use appropriate tools to give quantitative outcomes.

5. *Reward and correct*

   Managers must take responsibilities for guiding staff continuously with specific, timely feedback. Develop a schedule for managers to discuss indicators and outcome measures with staff frequently, and set targets accordingly. Frequent feedback on performance will prevent deficits from becoming serious. Request copies of unit (not individual) performance information.

How Much Change Occurred?

To assess the amount of change required comparable measures of evaluation criteria before and after training occurs. This requires trainers to decide—what criteria to use, how to measure them, and when to measure them.

Criteria

Actually, the choice of evaluation criteria occurs before training when instructional objectives are set because the two concepts are synonymous. Programmes are evaluated based on what the trainer sets out to do. Thus, relevant criteria include learning in terms of knowledge, attitudes, or skills; behavioural change on the job; and/or improvements or decrements in organizational results.

Measures

Learning can be measured using paper and pencil tests (for knowledge) questionnaires (for attitudes), or work sample tests (for skills). Behavioural change is assessed by means of such performance measures as indicators of individual output (e.g.; units produced or money sales) or one of the many forms of performance appraisal.

The ultimate measure in organizational results is utility, that is, an assessment of the money benefits accruing from such things as increased sales or reduced costs in comparison with the money costs of the programme.

Timing

Since evaluation is concerned with change, it follows that the appropriate criterion measures must be obtained both before and after the programme takes place. How much before and after varies with the type of measure(s) under consideration. Generally, assessments of knowledge, attitudes, and skills are obtained shortly before and immediately after the programme. Measures of job performance are taken from some typical period a few weeks or months before the programme and again a few weeks or months after trainees have returned to the job. Similarly, measures of organizational results are taken from some typical period a few weeks or months before the programme, but are not taken again until several months after trainees have returned to the job, since it typically will take a while before behavioural changes can be expected to result in, say, improved profits or reduced turnover.

Approaches to Training Evaluation

The first is called the before-and-after design, and the second is the time series design. The main difference is that in the former before and after measures of the evaluation criteria are taken only once each, and in the latter they are taken several times each. The advantage of the time series design is that it enables the evaluator to determine if there were upward or downward trends in the criterion measures before training that should be taken into account when assessing the programme's effect. One disadvantage is that the design is difficult to use for knowledge, attitudinal and skills criteria. (How many tests or questionnaires can trainees be expected to put up with?) A second disadvantage is the high costs of multiple measures.

Both the before-and -after and the time series approach show whether change has occurred, but neither can provide much assurance that the change is attributable to the training programme. The change could have resulted from a number of alternative factors, particularly alterations at the workplace.

Reasons for the Failure to Transfer of Training to the Job

When a company effectively develops a training programme it has to guarantee that trainees will apply their new knowledge or skills to the job setting. It has noted that only 10 per cent of the training information transfers to the job. Because improved job performance is the reason for giving training, such a lack of transfer renders a programme worthless. To transfer the training knowledge, the trainees must generalize the learned behaviour from the classroom to the job context and maintain those behaviours on the job. The failure to translate such training to job is due to the work environment, pressure of work, lack of supervisory support, etc. Certain other reasons for the trainees' failure to transfer their training are as follows:

1. Failure to learn the training material.
2. Inability to understand how to apply the training information to real life situations.
3. Lack of confidence in ones ability to perform the newly learned skills correctly.
4. Forgetting the material.
5. A temptation to go back to old, more familiar behaviours due to the trainees' unwillingness to take the time and effort necessary to integrate the new learned behaviours into existing behaviour patterns.

6. *Failure of development efforts to support enterprise objectives:* The purpose of training is to achieve enterprise objectives and develop professional managers. Unfortunately, there is little relationship between the training activities and the aim of the training.
7. *Emphasis on programme instead of result:* Some executives take pride in enrolling large number of employees for training. Benefits derived from attending these training are negligible unless they satisfy a clearly defined training need. Too often companies emphasize training activities with little concern for training results.
8. *Limiting the training for selected few:* An organization should send all employees for training and only chosen few should not be sent for training every time.

Suggestions to Ensure the Transfer of Training to the Job Setting

1. *Over learning:* For transfer to occur, training material must be learned and remembered. One way to ensure this is to provide the trainees with continued practice. The greater the over learning, greater the subsequent retention and transfer.
2. *Matching course content to the job:* This is to closely create a link between the training and job setting so that the trainees will understand how the learned material can be applied to the job setting. The use of examples like role-playing and computer simulations can help establish this linkage.
3. *Action plan:* A plan developed by trainees at the end of a training that indicates the steps they will take on the job to apply the new skills.
4. *Multiphase programme:* A training programme administered in several sessions in which trainees are given homework that requires them to apply that lesson back on the job and to discuss this experience during next training session.

5. *Performance devices:* Performance aids include checklist, decision tables, charts and diagrams that trainees use for guidance back on the job. They help them remember training material when they return to their jobs.
6. *Post-training follow up resources:* Follow up resources include a hotline number and instructor visits. A hotline number is one on which the instructor can be reached in case the trainees need advice about how to apply the training material on the job. The trainer may also visit the work spot to observe and assist the trainees as they apply learner behaviours.
7. *Building a supporting work environment:* Trainees' intentions to change their job behaviour cannot succeed without the support of their peers and supervisors. Trainer should also encourage the trainees' managers to create a supportive environment for the trainees.
8. *Maximize the similarity between training situations and work situations:* As far as possible, training situation and work situation must be undertaken in the same place or similar place.
9. *Provide adequate practice:* In addition to teaching theory, practice must be given to solve problems. On-the-job situations can be provided.
10. *Direct the trainees' attention to important aspects of the job:* When a trainee is undergoing training, in problem solving exercises, the crux of the issue must be dealt with in detail instead of beating-the-bush-round.

Summary

- Traditionally, training development functions have been rather lax in the measurement of the effectiveness of training. However, with reduced budgets it is even more important to measure the effectiveness of the training. It is now well recognized that at the start of any initiative the success criteria should be identified and the outcomes reviewed against this criteria.

- Evaluating leads to control, which mean deciding whether or not the training was worthwhile and what improvement are required to make it even more cost-effective. Evaluating is an integral feature of training.

Self-Learning Activity

Try to answer the following questions on your own:

1. Explain training effectiveness.
2. Discuss the techniques of training evaluation.
3. What are the failures to transfer training to the job?

20

INTERNATIONAL APPROACH TO TRAINING

In the era of globalization, training has crossed the boundaries and the sphere of training and training activities spread from one country to another country. The prominence of multinational corporations has led to the spreading of training activities from national level to international level. Where language barriers exist, such hurdles have been removed by means of interpreting and translating the training modules and techniques to local vernaculars and local conditions. When a training programme extends beyond a country, it saves lot of cost and time to the users. There is also scope for the free flow of ideas and innovations from one country to other country.

Preparations for International Approach to Training

When international approach is given to training, the following preparations need to be undertaken by an organization:

1. *Training needs analysis in various countries:* This is the basic information upon which subsequent training programmes and approaches would be structured. It should inventory the areas of 'knowledge' and 'skills' that the incumbents of the various areas of responsibility should possess. An attempt to codify the desirable 'attitudes' and

organizational ethos that the firm's top management wish to develop in the firm's personnel wherever they may be located would emerge during a structed dialogue with senior personnel. This is essentially international market research information upon which training plans will be based.

2. *'Input' analysis:* This is an important activity as the outcome of the analysis should identify with some clarity, what portion of the training can be handled in a standard format organized from a central vantage point and which training must be adapted to local needs. It pays to be thorough about this process, as mistakes at this stage can have an adverse effect on costs and on appropriateness.
3. *Define objectives and allocate responsibilities:* The analysis of the multi-country training needs should culminate in a clearly-defined set of objectives coupled with an allocation of responsibilities. Some of the needs could be best met by programmes organized at the 'centre' and obviously the responsibilities for this should rest with training resources at that location. Others must be delegated to local trainers.
4. *Establish a mechanism for co-ordination between 'centre' and 'field':* This is an area where many firms operating internationally fall down. If one believes in the 'brick-by-brick' approach it must be recognized that every component in the training system must be planned with an overall 'master plan'.
5. *Prepare programmer and select training methods:* Considerable thought should be given to the programme content and teaching methods. It must be born in mind that in an international organization there is often plenty of scope for a large number of exposures to a training module. The relatively high cost of preparing imaginative audio-visual learning packages can be absorbed more readily in a multinational people-intensive firm.

6. *Conduct training programmes and/or send participants on public courses:* Courses conducted by business schools or other training establishments often have an important role to play in a firm's overall training plans. However, it is important that such public courses/seminars/symposia/workshops are selected in response to clearly-defined training needs established during the research stage of the planning process.
7. *Evaluation of results:* Like any managerial activity, training must be subjected to control procedures with the aim of measuring how far the original aims have been met by international organisation. In an international organization such procedures should be designed with an eye for comparability inasmuch as qualitative responses to a questionnaire can suffer from cultural and linguistic variations. The ideal evacuation procedure, whenever possible, should incorporate short and sharp test papers where the answers to questions are unequivocal and directly related to learning messages that the programmer sought to impart.

Finally the cycle is completed with the evaluation data being fed back into the earlier stages of the training process. Gaps identified during this evaluation can be incorporated into future training plans and provide a most valuable 'input' for a continuous, dynamic training system.

Summary

- In the era of globalization, training has crossed the boundaries and the sphere of training and training activities spread from one country to another country. The prominence of multinational corporations has led to the spreading of training activities from national level to international level.

Self-Learning Activity

Try to answer the following questions on your own:

1. Discuss about input analysis for international approach to training.

Glossary

A

Action learning – A management development activity in which management gives candidates real problems to solve.

Apprenticeship training – A structured process by which people become skilled workers through a combination of classroom teaching and on-the-job training.

B

Behaviour modelling – A training method in which the trainees are shown how a task should be performed and then practice the task with feedback until they are competent.

C

Case method – A training method in which a trainee is presented with a written description of an organizational problem to diagnose to solve.

Change related training – Training that enables employees to keep up-to-date with various types of changes dealing with technological advances or a change in the organization's strategic plan.

Computer-based instruction (CBI) – A training method that uses a computer to instruct trainees through tutorials, games, and simulations.

Critical incident method (CIT) – A systematic method of recording job analysis information that identifies specific work behavior that determines success or failure in executing an assigned task.

D

Designing training programme – It denotes the strategy and planning through which training programmes could be conducted effectively.

G

Group brainstorming – A technique of demand for costing in which a panel of experts generates a forecast in collaboration.

H

Human capital – The knowledge, education, training, skills, and expertise of a firm's workers.

J

Job analysis – A systematic procedure for gathering, analyzing, and documenting information about particular jobs.

Job description – A list of job's duties, responsibilities, working conditions, and supervisory responsibilities — one product of job analysis.

Job enlargement – Assigning workers additional same level activities, thus increasing the number of activities they perform.

Job enrichment – Re-designing jobs in a way that increases the opportunities for the worker to experience feelings of responsibility, achievement and recognition.

Job evaluation – A systematic process of determining worth of a job

Job instruction training (JIT) – Listing each job's basic tasks, along with key points in order to provide step-by-step training for employees.

Job rotation – A method of management development in which companies rotate trainees through a number of departments.

Job specification – A list of job's human requirements that is, the requisite education, skills, personality, and so on — another product of job analysis.

L

Lecture – A training method in which the trainer teaches a topic by verbally communicating the information.

M

Management game – A development technique in which teams of managers compete by making computerized decisions regarding realistic but simulated situations.

Mentoring – Experienced supervisors, who are assigned to new managers to teach, guide, advise, and serve as role models.

Multiple training programme – A training programme administered in several sessions in which trainees are given homework that requires them to apply the lesson by on-the-job and to discuss this experience during the next training session.

O

On-the-job training – A training method in which trainees are taught how to perform their jobs in the actual job setting.

Orientation training – Training designed to inform new employees about their jobs, the company, and its policies and procedures.

Over learning – Learning training material so well that it will be long remembered, even without frequent practice.

P

Position analysis questionnaire – A systematic method of recording job analysis information in which the behavioral dimension of a job are specified.

Programmed learning – A systematic method of teaching job skills involving presenting questions or facts allowing the persons to respond and giving the learner immediate feedback.

R

Rater effectiveness training (RET) – Performance appraisal training that teaches raters the meaning of each performance.

Remedial training – Training designed to correct deficiencies in employee skill or knowledge levels or to improve employee attitudes.

Role-playing – A training technique in which trainees act out parts in a realistic management situation.

S

Sensitivity training – A method for increasing employees' insight into their own behavior by discussions in groups led by special trainers.

Simulated training – Training employees on special off-the-job equipment.

T

Training – The process of teaching new employees the basic skills they need to perform their jobs.

Training evaluation – An assessment of the effectiveness of a training programme.

Training need – A problem that can be rectified through training.

Training objectives – Statements describing what the trainee should be able to do as the result of training.

Team building – Improving the effectiveness of teams through the use of consultants and team building meetings.

V

VERJAS - Versatile Job Analysis System – A systematic method of recording job analysis information regarding functions, tasks, job context, and worker requirements.

References

Adiar J. (1987) *Effective Team Building*, London, Pan Books.

Bass B. (1966) *Training in Industry*, London, Tavistock Publications.

Bailey D. (1998) *The Training Handbook*, London, Gee Publishing.

Bartman (1997) *Training Needs Analysis*, Aldershot, Grower.

Ball C., et. al. (1994) *Promoting Lifelong Career Development*, Cambridge, CRAC.

Barrington H. (1997) *Training Interventions*, Institute of Personnel and Development.

Bebbin M. (1981) *Management Teams - Why they succeed or Fail*, London, Heinenmann.

Bentley T. (1990) *The Business of Training*, Maiden Head, McGraw Hill.

Branby P. (1996) *Evaluation of Training Effectiveness*, Maiden Head, McGraw Hill.

Bishop S. (1995) *25 Role Plays*, Aldershot, Grower.

Burke J. (1998) *Competency Based Education and Training*, London, Falmer Press.

Carroll (1997) *Handbook of Counseling*, London, Sage.

Carter S. (1994) *An Essential Guide to Mentoring*, London, Institute of Management.

Craig R. (1967) *Training and Development Handbook*, New York, McGraw Hill.

David K. (1964) *Training within the Organization*, London, Travistock Publishers.

Davis M. (1989) *Active Role Play*, London, Blackwell.

Dowens S. (1995) *Learning at Work*, London, Kogan-Page.

Elgood (1997) *Handbook of Management Games*, Aldershot, Grower.

Graham RG (1969) *Business Games Handbook*, New York, American Management Association.

George A. (1997) *Train and Develop Yourself*, Aldershot, Grower.

George Odiorne (1970) *Training by Objectives*, New York, MacMillan.

Goldstein I. (1992) *Training in Organizations*, New York, Brooks Cole.

Harrison R. (1989) *Training and Development*, London, IPM.

Hay J. (1992) *Transactional Analysis for Trainer*, Maiden Head, McGraw Hill.

Honey P. (1996) *The Manual of Learning Styles*, Maiden Head, Peter Honey Publishers

ILO, No. 4, *Human Relations - Case Studies and Role Playing*.

ILO, (1986) *An Introductory Course in Training Methods for Management Development*.

ILO, No. 27, *An Introduction to Business Games*.

Jones S. (1996) *Developing a Learning Culture*, Maiden Head, McGraw Hill.

Jones K. (1987) *Simulations — A Handbook*, London, Kogan Page.

Jones K. (1988) *Interactive Learning Events*, London, Kogan Page.

Koble D. (1984) *Experimental Learning*, Prentice Hall.

Ladourse GP (1987) *Role Play*, Oxford, OUP.

MacGill I. (1992) *Action Learning*, London, Kogan Page

MacLennan N. (1995) *Coaching and Mentoring*, Aldershot, Grower.

Megginson D. (1996) *Cultivating Self-Development*, London, IPD.

Newby AC (1994) *Training Evaluation Handbook*, Aldershot, Grower.

Norton & Burt (1997) *Practicing Self-Development*, Corby, Institute of Management.

Parsloe E. (1993) *Coaching, Mentoring, and Assessing*, London, Kogan Page.

Patton MQ (1997) *Utilization of Focused Evaluation*, London, Sage.

Parker G. (1996) *Team Players and Team Work*, Prentice Hall.

Pedler M. (1997) *Action Learning in Practice*, Aldershot, Grower.

Revans B. (1980) *Action Learning*, London, Blond & Briggs.

Rae L. (1992) *Guide to In-Company Training Methods*, Aldershot, Grower.

Rae L. (1997) *How to Measure Training Effectiveness*, Aldershot, Grower.

Rae L. (1997) *Planning and Designing Training Programmes*, Aldershot, Grower.

Sloman MA (1994) *Handbook of Training Strategy*, Aldershot, Grower.

Stuart I. (1988) T*A Today*, Lifespace Publishing.

Taylor B. (1975) *Management Development and Training Handbook*, London, McGraw Hill.

Tracy W. (1971) *Designing Training and Development Systems*, American Management Association.

Wills M. (1998) *Managing the Training Process*, Aldershot, Grower.

Witmore J. (1992) *Coaching for Performance*, London, Nicholas Barley.

Yardley KM (1997) *Role Play — Theory and Practice*, London, Sage.

INDEX